Public Sector Privatization

Recent Titles from Quorum Books

PUBLIC SECTOR PRIVATIZATION

Alternative Approaches to Service Delivery

Edited by **Lawrence K. Finley**

QUORUM BOOKS
New York • Westport, Connecticut • London

RECEIVED

APR 1   1991

Kennedy School
Library

Library of Congress Cataloging-in-Publication Data

Public sector privatization : alternative approaches to service
  delivery / edited by Lawrence K. Finley.
      p. cm.
    Includes index.
    Bibliography: p.
    ISBN 0-89930-330-7 (lib. bdg. : alk. paper)
    1. Contracting out—United States. 2. Privatization—United
States. I. Finley, Lawrence K.
  HD3861.U6P83   1989
  338.973—dc19   88-36486

British Library Cataloguing in Publication Data is available.

Library of Congress Catalog Card Number: 88-36486
ISBN: 0-89930-330-7

First published in 1989 by Quorum Books

Greenwood Press, Inc.
88 Post Road West, Westport, Connecticut 06881

Printed in the United States of America

The paper used in this book complies with the
Permanent Paper Standard issued by the National
Information Standards Organization (Z39.48-1984).

10 9 8 7 6 5 4 3 2 1

This book is dedicated
with love
to
Rita, Paula, Laura, and Jason

Contents

Preface

Governments are responsible for deciding which services citizens want provided publicly and then providing (authorizing, empowering, administering) them at levels for which the citizens are willing to pay. Of those services desired from a government, part can be best produced or delivered by that government, while many others can be delivered better by alternative means.

In this book researchers and administrators present models and experience bearing on service delivery choices. When I first embarked on this writing and editorial venture, I intended to locate and induce the most qualified and balanced team of individuals available to write on topics previously chosen as the next decade's "hot topics" within the broad area of service delivery alternatives. In large part I am happy with the result. Unfortunately correctional services are omitted, as are "private goods," such as food, delivered by governments. As for balance, eight chapters are by publicly employed persons while four are by people in private employment. As one would expect, those whose livelihoods more directly depend on these choices seem to be more "caught up" in the issues, while those of us whose livelihoods are insulated from the choices can be a bit detached.

Part One of the book is introductory, providing dimensions of public services, changes, and alternative delivery. Chapters 1 and 2 overview alternate methods of delivering public services.

Chapter 1 poses the broad question: How shall complex organizations in changing environments be managed? Adaptation must become the central concern of public decision makers. Alternative delivery is driven by the requirement to adapt. This chapter clarifies language to facilitate further communication. A survey of alternative service delivery is presented, along with potential advantages and shortcomings of each. Criteria by which decision makers might select producers are cost and effectiveness.

Chapter 2, by Lydia Manchester of International City Managers Association in Washington, DC, provides an inside view of alternative service delivery. She focuses on opportunities for service improvement at the city level. From her viewpoint of extensive association with city managers she reports their perspectives on cost, effectiveness, dependability, and other criteria. She reflects city managers' concern with maintaining public control over services, as opposed to a pure privatizer's interest in switching control to private parties.

In Chapter 3, Ed Doherty, Environmental Services Commissioner in Rochester, New York, describes the situation that led to greatly expanded contracting in Rochester in the late 1970s. He presents an inventory of contracts in use along with estimated annual cost saving in five program categories. Cost impacts of contracting are analyzed. Next he evaluates service effectiveness based on criteria of satisfaction (complaints), usage, response to emergency, and policy control. Finally, personnel issues associated with contracting are identified. Rochester manages alternative service delivery in a labor union environment.

The experience of an unusual city is presented in Chapter 4. Bruce Janken, City Coordinator, and Betsy Conrad, City Clerk, write about Florence, Kentucky. First is a description of the city, with emphasis on its phenomenal growth and large, experienced neighbors. These become main factors in the delivery of services in Florence, and both contribute to the decision to contract for services rather than produce them. Service contracting with other government units is the second part of the chapter. Third are services contracted to private producers.

Part Two, Focusing on Services, begins with Chapter 5, an analysis of environmental infrastructure alternatives. This business perspective is by Philip Giantris, previously with Metcalf and Eddy, Inc., and now President and General Manager of Bird Environmental Systems, Inc., in South Walpole, Massachusetts. He discusses full service privatization and contract operations and maintenance. Successes at four cities are described. Criteria in selecting a private infrastructure producer are expertise, experience, and dedicated resources.

Chapter 6, "Privatization of Transportation Services," is by Roger F. Teal, Civil Engineering Professor at the University of California, Irvine. He describes three alternative means of highway development; private developers, taxes, and tolls. Four cities now have toll-financed highways and probably would have otherwise gone without these roads. The situation bringing about Urban Mass Transportation Administration's privatization efforts was extreme cost increases in subsidized monopoly transit. Competitive bidding is often an unattainable objective of federal privatization policy, despite studies showing a mean savings of 27 percent by private operators. Transit unions stand to lose, and so pose formidable barriers to more efficient service.

Chapter 7 is by John Turner, former Vice President of Rural/Metro Corporation, Scottsdale, Arizona. This is a colorful account of forty years as a private fire protection contractor. Rural/Metro now derives more revenues from ambulance operations than any other source, followed by fire protection, home health care, and security. The company was sold to its employees in 1978. Battles for business with public employee unions continue to thwart alternative fire protection.

Chapter 8 is the first of two chapters on alternative health care delivery. Health Care Professor Wayne Higgins, Western Kentucky University, analyzes the economic forces changing health care. Demand growth, regulation, reform attempts, insurance, managed care, and vertical integration are evaluated in a careful, scholarly manner. Higgins offers balanced perspective and progressive policy recommendations.

Chapter 9 relates the perspective and experience of Humana, Inc., contracting with the former Old General public hospital in Louisville, Kentucky. In 1983 Humana agreed to lease the facility, deliver medical services and education programs, and to treat indigent as well as private patients. This partnership is a model for other troubled hospitals across the country. Ingredients for successful turnarounds are recognized need, corporate ability to operate with minimal interference, and strong commitment by government, university, and private sector to make the partnership and indigent care work.

Part Three, Constraints and Opportunities, begins with Chapter 10, a discussion by attorney Mark Flener of three areas of law with which decision makers in public and private capacities should be familiar. First is government's legal liabilities when contracting out and how those liabilities may be limited. Second is an overview of financial responsibilities of contracting entities and what happens if an entity cannot perform as promised. The third topic is government financing of facilities through bonds, and the roles of the bond attorney.

Chapter 11 is my recommended process by which businessmen and women can develop an entry wedge and begin to compete with public deliverers. Experience effects, specialization of labor, and new technology often mean that private companies have competitive advantages over public producers. There remains the problem of targeting services and locations to pursue. The privatizer is urged to indentify decision makers and their interests carefully and then seek to market private service possibilities generally and her own services in particular, in a two-stage process.

Chapter 12 transports us far from the previous material by giving us an insight into privatization in Western Europe. In Europe privatization tends to be denationalization, but Professor van Oudenhoven, of the University of Groningen, Netherlands, gives us a glimpse at local services as well. The goals of Europeans are broadly the same as those in the United States: cost reduction, efficiency, and innovation, all through competition. The 1980s will be known as the decade of the market in Europe. At the local level, police surveillance is contracted by more than thirty cities. Private financing of infrastructure, toll roads, contracted garbage collection, and volunteer nursing are found in Europe.

Acknowledgments

For information and inspiration helpful in compiling this book I thank the following individuals: Gabriel Buntzman, Edgar Busch, Kim Carter Parker, Carl Chelf, William Davis, Dean Garrett, Thomas Gannon, Brian Goff, Charles Hardcastle, Jerry Kinard, Stephen Lile, Barbara Mandeville, Kirby Ramsey, and Julie Ward.

Additionally, appreciation is felt for the assistance of unknown people who researched, drafted, typed, and proofread material.

PART ONE

ISSUES IN ALTERNATIVE SERVICE DELIVERY

1

Alternative Service Delivery, Privatization, and Competition

LAWRENCE K. FINLEY

Action that has many elements and forces interacting in various ways is said to be complex. Public services are complex and continually changing. Because they are also important to most of us, they also require and deserve careful decisions.

As an example of the complexity let us consider public safety. It is said to be provided in a neighborhood by a city council's decision and arrangements for safety/security-trained persons to patrol the streets regularly and otherwise deter criminal or unsafe behaviors. County, state, and federal officials are also elements. Each government has its own separate but overlapping responsibilities, laws, constituents, and special expertise.

Security needs are met—security is produced or delivered—when safety security/actions are taken that reduce unsafe/insecure behaviors. Production may be accomplished in limitless ways, from police to volunteers, from high fences and gates to electronic surveillance. Even a real estate developer's decision to locate new housing in a low-crime area, families' habits, parents' teachings, and employment opportunities all have significant impact on the security of people and property. Note that both provision and delivery of security is both public and private. And safety/security is but a fraction of public services. So we see that "public service" is a complex concept.

Not only is the field complex, but it is continually changing. Governments add services here and shed services there. This year a city contracts with a neighbor city for a service it has always hired a private company to perform. Facilities in dire condition, which once would have been repaired, may now face replacement or may be sold. Federal support waxes and wanes. Yuppies, dinks, and underemployeds balloon. Droughts and politics threaten us. That fundamental changes have occurred in the provision and production of public services in the past twenty years is not disputed.

Do we know how to manage change and complexity well? Do we as members of a nation, states, counties, and cities have better lives because of these changes? Who benefits when a piece of government-owned property is sold to individuals?

Who has the greatest stakes in the level and method of trash collection and disposal? Are alternative ways of producing street repairs more efficient, or do they just use lower-cost labor? If only we had Solomon's wisdom to know with certainty the answers to these questions!

But in a complex, changing organizational environment, decision makers must adapt to uncertainty. Adapting to uncertainty is so central for organizations that it has been the major theme in the study of organizations for close to three decades now (Burns and Stalker, 1961; Lawrence and Lorsch, 1969). What kind of uncertainty are we talking about? Managers often cannot predict whether a budget is feasible, whether investments of training time and money will generate a return, whether constituents will be pleased by a change in service levels, whether a new bidder will live up to a contractor's expectations.

Lacking definitive answers, one tries to learn while muddling through, trying a new contract clause here, sticking with an acceptable maintenance procedure there. Managers must draw information and perspectives from many people. So they add to their knowledge and understanding by watching, listening, arguing, and reading. The advantage of the written word, especially a book, is that the writers have had time to be thoughtful and careful, and to draw on the best from others in a way the other sources have not.

To approach the questions we want answered, we first define central terms and map the territory. Objectives and criteria by which to evaluate service claims and outcomes need to be understood and are discussed later.

Public services are *provided* (decided on, arranged for) for some public. Public providers are those with legislative capacity to acquire money. School districts, water authorities, towns, cities, states, and nations are public providers. Publics receiving benefits of these monies ideally coincide with the payers. However, there is usually not a perfect coincidence—not even in the private sector, and certainly not in the public sector. Thus a city decides to provide traffic safety, collects money from property owners, employers, and employees, then directs that money primarily to travelers on certain streets within its borders. Or a state collects income taxes across its entire work force, then builds a marketing cooperative facility to serve only farmers in a few counties. Often there is not a close match between those paying for a service and those receiving it.

There is no limit to the range of services a public (government) will provide somewhere, sometime. In theory there are certain goods and services that should be public and others that should be private. And certain individuals need publicly provided services while others can provide for themselves. In practice the most private good, such as chocolate pie, is often publicly provided to the most able, such as an executive. This occurs in government-owned commercial establishments in or near the seats of government, universities, and other agencies.

Services most commonly provided publicly are defense, safety (including crime prevention, fire prevention, traffic control, various inspections), transportation ways, parks, recreation, health, and education. The main thing these so called *public goods* have in common is positive externalities, benefits accruing to those external to the immediate beneficiary group. For example, if Hoosiers provided for their defense from foreign aggression, Kentuckians could "ride free." Or if your close neighbor provided for fire prevention, you would also benefit. And if you live in an educated society, you benefit even though you may be uneducated or educated in another society. Especially if nonpayers (free riders) cannot be excluded from enjoying certain services, these services are logical candidates to be publicly provided, at the expense of all taxpayers.

Often user need is said to be a sufficient reason to provide publicly. To say that needs should be met by public welfare services, however, is to substitute a provider's values (public choices) for the recipient's. That is, if one is judged to need housing but spends substantially at the track, clearly there is a problematic difference in choices. Clearly in a money economy all mentally competent people need money. Provision of money—ignoring the problem of choice differences—to those who cannot provide for themselves is not a service delivery problem but a problem solved by reversing the government's money collection activity. This is best thought of as a tax issue, since it would be regressive taxation in extreme.

Neither provision of services nor distribution of monies is a main concern of this book. Although this book is eclectic, it focuses on alternative delivery or production of services. The public versus private delivery choice is paramount, but choices between two public providers are also presented. The text is written largely by individuals who have management experience in alternative delivery or who have studied the choices impartially. Hopefully no writer for this book would recommend one means of producing a public service if another means appeared to meet accepted criteria better.

Having identified the service and provider dimensions of the choices, we turn to production (delivery) means. Kolderie (1986) argues that security, for example, can be provided and produced either publicly or privately. The relationships can be shown graphically with a matrix (see next page).

Most interest in privatization in the United States is in production (delivery) of services. There is limited interest in private provision, except among committed conservatives. We will now identify main publicly delivered services and then the alternatives for delivering these services.

Public employees are the most common means of delivering national defense, state education and penal service, city-county cemetery services, safety patrols, fire prevention, and recreational services (Valente and Manchester, 1984).

	Publicly	Privately
Privately	North Star Hockey team decides and contracts with city police	Department store decides for security and employs Pinkertons
Publicly	State writes law, collects and appropriates money, builds and operates prison	City decides for security at hockey game and hires Pinkertons

Services Provided (arranged for)

           Publicly   **Privately**

**Services Produced
(Delivered)**

Note that even these seemingly simple statements are actually misleading. National defense actually comes from a strong economy in the United States and natural barriers in Switzerland. Fire prevention occurs every time a person hides the matches from children or buys a smoke alarm. These phenomena are difficult or impossible to measure in surveys. So governments are surveyed or otherwise observed to see whether they still provide traditional services or whether alternatives are being used.

ALTERNATIVES

Contracting to private organizations is by far the most common alternative to production of services by public employees (Ferris and Graddy, 1986). A government and a company or other organization agree that the company will produce (deliver) stated services, and in consideration the government will pay an amount or rate of money. The government collects money and decides what services it will support, at what level, to whom, where, when, and how all these specifications will be ensured. In situations (usually tangible services) where specifications can be clearly written and performance well monitored, it would seem that public officials have an obligation, first, to determine the trade-off between cost and effectiveness (service level choice) and then determine whether the best producer is the organization in which they hold office or another available party. Whether an alternative producer is public or private is not as important as its effectiveness and efficiency.

Franchising is a special contract or agreement. Franchisees are different from other contracting parties in that they collect the money from the recipients of the service. Franchises are used in situations where the government determines that only one or a few producers should have the legal right to offer the service in a particular geographic area. This determination may be made because economies of scale mean that one large provider will be most efficient, as in the case of cable TV, waste collection, airport services, and utilities. Franchises are sometimes used because providers should meet certain tests of character, as in the case of liquor stores. (Exclusive franchises or licenses may be felt appropriate, so that the money collection is more palatable than it would be if collected by the government, though this is not an ethical reason to franchise.)

Any or all these situations may call for franchising as an alternate delivery means. One should note that whereas competition in "free markets" is continual, competition in the case of franchises is limited to the period in which the exclusive right to produce the service is acquired. By definition, once the exclusive right is obtained there is no competition until the franchise period expires.

Parenthetically, exclusive franchises in the private sector often run afoul of antitrust laws, which prohibit actions that adversely affect competition. Thus, on the one hand we have a tradition of disallowing anticompetitive behavior dating back almost a century, while on the other hand we grant public franchises whose effect is to exclude potential competitors from markets. Decision makers must make trade-offs between benefits of competition and benefits of scale economies or public control.

Beyond these three ways publicly provided services are produced are other practices meriting examination. Subsidies and incentives to private producers, vouchers, and voluntary and self-help efforts are ways governments often involve private parties in public service.

Subsidies and incentives are provision efforts, not production. For example, governments may decide what to provide, how much, to whom, and by whom, and then encourage chosen services by subsidies. These incentives to producers obviously increase supply, but less obviously also increase consumption by lowering costs and therefore prices. For example, subsidies (or incentives) may be awarded to a commuter bus company, a nonprofit health clinic or school, or a for-profit tobacco producer. Paradoxically a government may simultaneously discourage (through heavy taxation) smoking, drinking whiskey, and other behaviors. The intent is not to be sarcastic, but to point out the lack of consistency of some subsidies and incentives. Hopefully governments will not waste resources and lower public confidence by working at cross purposes.

Incentives often take the form of tax abatement or preference for the purpose of stimulating job creation. Recent decades have witnessed urban renewal, model cities, Urban Development Action Grants (UDAG), and other programs to throw a lifeline to seemingly helpless inner cities (Butler, 1982). Enterprise zones, a 1970s departure from 1960s urban renewal programs, were tax waivers designed to attract and expand job-creating investments in disadvantaged neighborhoods, mostly in inner cities. Evidence suggests that tax waivers alone are ineffective in attracting private investment and only slightly more effective at stimulating expansion of existing businesses there (Morse and Farmer, 1986).

The more important action has been job training (Beam, 1987). IBM, Xerox, and a few other companies have good track records in job training, but most companies currently find high schools, vocational schools, and colleges better equipped to deliver this service. To the extent that severe unemployment in inner cities is unacceptable in our advanced society, the public has a role in job creation.

An increasingly common incentive is used for industrial recruitment. Broader than the enterprise zone concept, these relocation or expansion incentive packages appear to be public provision run amuck. Companies that intend to locate somewhere in the United States find themselves offered megabucks by competing governments. The escalation of these inducements is phenomenal. Nissan's truck plant in Tennessee cost taxpayers $11,000 per job created in 1980 (Milward and Newman, 1988). Recent job creation by Toyota and by Fuji-Isuzu cost taxpayers approximately $50,000 per job. Proponents argue that supplier factories and service jobs flow from the initial factory, justifying the public investment. Critics argue that governments are playing a negative sum game. The companies would build somewhere without induce-ments, and so considered from a national perspective, there is no net payoff. In fact there is a large net cost. Of course, so long as one government (state, county, or city) offers incentives, rivals must do it to get their share of new jobs. Perhaps federal legislation is needed.

Vouchers are a special case of reverse collection of money. Whereas negative tax money can be used by the recipient for any purpose, a voucher must be used for the purpose chosen by a government. Both may be available to only selected (needy) recipients. While vouchers do not give the recipient a choice of services, they do carry a choice of producers of the service.

Producers are usually private but could include competing public bodies. Certainly a primary thrust of vouchers is to encourage competing producers of the service the government chooses to partially provide. Where user choice and producer competition are necessary to ensure expected quality of service, then vouchers make sense.

Volunteers are increasingly used by governments, churches, hospitals, and individuals to provide nursing or shopping or clothing services. These volunteers are typically given training and then scheduled or matched with service recipients. Cost saving is usually the impetus when government does not rely on paid workers. However, Hospice and perhaps other organizations may feel that monetary pay would attract people with less desirable motives and encourage less desired behaviors.

Privatization is another alternative delivery option term that we need to examine. Referring to the matrix, we define privatization as any change from public toward private provision or production of services. Thus contracting out to a company for services previously produced by publicly employed persons is privatization while contracting out to another government is alternative delivery (production) but not privatization. This distinction between privatization and alternative delivery is important because the willingness to contract out, whether to a private company or to another government, introduces competition to the arena. Comparing bids, proposals, or actual performance records of two or more producers means competition and probably stimulates better performance.

Competition—struggle or rivalry for a prize—can be one of the strongest impetuses toward effectiveness and efficiency. People would be competing for jobs—their own or others'—if a city considered a company or another city as an alternate producer of any service. Franchising is usually to a private company, but could be to another government, and perhaps should be if one is nearby and its employees want the opportunity.

Any action that encourages the formation of a new rival producer, strengthens a weak rival, or weakens a dominant rival increases competition. Any action that discourages formation of a new rival, weakens an already weak producer, or strengthens a dominant one reduces competition.

When a government subsidizes a private health clinic (via Medicare, for example) or a private school (by offering student grants), privatization of delivery occurs, since the private organization substitutes for a public one. Thus a subsidy may strengthen or weaken competition (result in more or less viable alternatives) depending on the status of the recipient organization. Vouchers, on the other hand, always increase competition, since alternatives are always encouraged. To a pragmatic decision maker competition (strong alternatives) is more important than whether the alternatives are public or private.

Privatization in Europe and to a lesser extent in the United States is occurring as assets, usually physical facilities, are sold to private buyers. When government-owned companies are sold, rights to use established brand names, customer lists, patents, and other intangible or intellectual property are transferred. More important than ownership per se is privatization of provision and production of "private" services. Conrail is the main instance of such privatization in the United States. Mass transportation has historically been publicly produced in many countries, of course, only recently becoming "denationalized." In many of these instances we do not see a greater number of viable alternative producers, although we see government getting out of "private goods."

From Benjamin Franklin's day until recently, letter and parcel delivery had been predominantly public in the United States. Federal Express, United Parcel Service, Airborne Express, and numerous smaller companies are busily privatizing this large and still-growing domain of services. This change appears to be primarily caused by user choice, although the U.S. Postal Service seems ambivalent about enforcement of its exclusive franchise as a letter carrier. The important point is that alternative delivery does not always depend upon government policy. When a heretofore public service is ineffectively or inefficiently performed, a private market may be developed by entrepreneurs. Private demand will be met by supply as long as there are entrepreneurs (Finley, 1990).

CRITERIA

Alternative delivery suggests choices, and choices suggest a need to think about service objectives and criteria. The first criterion in the public's mind is probably, "What will I give up to provide X service?" That is, what will the service cost if it is delivered in alternative ways? Obvious costs associated with alternative delivery are the tax money collected and paid to contractors (or paid directly by recipients to franchisees), or as subsidy, funds for vouchers, and so on. Additionally, costs of soliciting bids and proposals, of choosing providers, fees to accountants and lawyers, and costs of monitoring performance must be included.

On the other hand, if the service is kept in-house, there would still be costs of considering alternatives, monitoring performance, and significant opportunity costs. Generally a government fails to consider opportunity costs in its decision process. For example, if public production of a maintenance service entails owning a $1 million (market value) warehouse on a piece of real estate that has appreciated to $2 million, then at a 10 percent rate of interest and 1 percent tax rate, there is a $300,000 annual opportunity cost of public ownership plus $30,000 lost property tax. While these are not accounting, out-of-pocket costs, they should be included when counting costs to choose among alternative delivery sources.

The first criterion in the service recipient's mind is, reasonably, quality or effectiveness of the service. Determining service quality and deciding how much quality to buy are important roles of public administrators and elected officials, respectively. Ideally *output* quality requirements are specified, such as gallons of water furnished per day meeting health department standards or snow on X streets and roads cleared with X minutes of notification of need. Unfortunately, quality may only be stated in *inputs*, such as X number of water pumps or X snowplows used. Using output standards shifts risk to the producer and reasonably merits higher prices.

Credentials are a creeping form of input standard widely used in endeavors of intangible, difficult-to-specify performance such as health, education, recreation, and the arts. Nevertheless competency or past performance is worth examining as a possible criterion substitute for high-cost credentials.

A misconception is that service quality is a constant—it is either present or absent. In fact quality in every service is a variable, often inseparable from service level, and it can usually be bought in increments. Even safety and health are "economic goods," as interstate highways and modern hospitals demonstrate. That is, we can always save or prolong more lives with more money.

The cost of quality often is described by an upward sloping curve. For example, to staff a health clinic so that average patient waiting time is cut from forty-five minutes to twenty-five minutes may cost an additional $100 per day. However, to cut average waiting time from twenty-five to five minutes might cost another $1,000 daily. This large change in cost per unit of quality occurs in the illustration because of the unpredictable nature of the arrival pattern of patients, causing the clinic to have a staff for the period of heaviest load and therefore have unused staff the majority of time. This cost behavior means that the public office holders and managers must avoid the enticing trap of promising perfect services.

SUMMARY

Complexity and change in public service lead to decision-making uncertainty. In this environment adaptive governments are needed, managed by informed decision makers. Alternate service delivery opportunities today mean that "business as usual" is no longer acceptable. Public goods may be provided by cities and other governments, but providing and delivering are often independent. Contracting, franchising, and encouraging services through incentives, subsidies, and vouchers are evaluated as alternate service delivery means. Privatization is a change toward private provision or delivery and is only one way of generating alternatives. Competition is an important incentive and is a main advantage of alternate delivery opportunities. Criteria by which service deliveries should be evaluated and selected are primarily cost and quality (efficiency and effectiveness). Output rather than input standards are recommended. Quality costs increase at an increasing rate; therefore decision makers must realistically avoid the mistake of promising perfect services.

REFERENCES

Beam, Alex (1987, February 16). "Why Few Ghetto Factories Are Making It." *Business Week*, pp. 88-89.

Burns, T., and Stalker, G. M. (1961). *The Management of Innovation*. London: Tavistock.

Butler, Stuart M. (1982). "The Enterprise Zone as a Political Animal." *Cato Journal* 2, 373-385.

Ferris, J., and Graddy, E. (1986). Contracting Out: For What? With Whom? *Public Administration Review*, 46, 332-344.

Finley, Lawrence K. (1990). *Entrepreneurial Strategies*. Boston: PWS-Kent.

Kolderie, T. (1986). The Two Different Concepts of Privatization. *Public Administration Review*, 46, 285-291.

Lawrence, P. R., and Lorsch, J. W. (1969). *Organization and Environment: Managing Differentiation and Integration*. Homewood, IL: Irwin.

Milward, H. Brinton, and Heidi Hosbach Newman (1988). *State Incentive Packages and the Industrial Location Decision*. Center for Business and Economic Research, University of Kentucky, Lexington, KY.

Morse, George W., and Farmer, Michael C. (1986). "Location and Investment Effects of a Tax Abatement Program," *National Tax Journal,* 39, 229-236.

Valente, C. F. and Manchester, L. D. (1984). "Rethinking Local Services: Examining Alternative Delivery Services." *Management Information Service Special Report number 12.* Washington, DC: International City Managers Association.

2

Alternative Service Delivery Approaches and City Service Planning

LYDIA MANCHESTER

WHAT IS ALTERNATIVE SERVICE DELIVERY?

The definition of alternative service delivery methods has been the topic of a lively discussion for more than a decade now. Many of the first authors used the term *privatization* for an array of activities such as abandonment of services, public-private partnerships, productivity improvements elicited as a result of private corporations such as loaned executives, and alternative delivery approaches such as contracting. There remains little consensus today as to the meaning of these terms.

This chapter will focus on those delivery options where the government continues to have some *direct* involvement in the design, selection, level, and financing of a service. This chapter will not discuss in detail complete abandonment of a service by a local government (sometimes referred to as service shedding) or the sale of assets or other financial arrangements with the private sector. The discussion will focus on alternative service delivery methods, such as contracting and volunteers, in which the local government uses someone other than local employees (a private company, nonprofit organization, or individual) to deliver the service, *but* the service continues to be available in the community and the community retains some control over its delivery and price. However, the local government always retains the responsibility for providing the service, including the regulation of the quality and cost of the service.

Providing a service entails deciding that it will be made available and arranging for its delivery. This is an integral part of a local government's policymaking process. It is up to the council, with input from the community and staff, to determine the scope and level of services that are to be available in the community. For example, some communities may regard arts and cultural services as entirely within the domain of the private sector; others might view the enhancement of the arts as an important part of the improvement in the community's quality of life. How much health care, job training, recreation services, and transportation to provide is part of the policy decision about services in the community.

Delivering a service is actually producing the service (for example, picking up the trash, sweeping the streets, providing counseling, operating the library). Although a local government may decide that it wants to provide a service as part of its community mission or vision, it does not necessarily have to be the service deliverer. It may choose instead one or more alternative delivery options to limit its involvement to ensuring that the service is available in the community. In such instances, the community is still involved in the payment for these services (to the contractor) and the oversight of the delivery. The local government is not getting out of the business of providing the service, but rather has arranged to have the service available in the community and will continue to have responsibility for service oversight. The alternative service delivery options are a means of improving productivity and cost effectiveness by using a service provider that can deliver the service more efficiently than local employees.

WHY FOCUS ON ALTERNATIVE SERVICE DELIVERY?

We have said that in this chapter we would focus only on alternative service delivery methods as a means of clarifying the definitions of privatization, public-private partnership, and so on. Part of the reason is that privatization is often a misleading and overly politicized term. For most people, privatization means that the private sector has assumed full responsibility for the delivery and financing of a service; the public sector has abdicated all responsibility. This is what has been discussed most frequently at the federal and international levels.

The federal government, in implementing its privatization efforts, has chosen not to continue to have any direct involvement in the activities that are privatized because the policymakers' vision of what the federal government should be delivering does not include these services. Thus, they are making a policy decision about the types and level of services to be delivered by the federal government. In part, these decisions to privatize are also based upon a decision to limit competition between the private and public sectors. If private providers exist, the federal government has determined that it should not be competing with these companies with public delivery.

But is this same discussion and privatization activity taking place at the local level? A recent survey conducted by International City Managers Association (ICMA) in conjunction with Touche Ross and the Privatization Council seems to indicate no. Only a small number of communities were found to be getting out of the service "business" for any services. These activities usually involved the one-time sale of a surplus asset (such as the sale of a school building no longer needed by the community) rather than a decision to reduce services to the public. There is considerably more evidence of local governments using alternative service delivery approaches as a means to improve productivity and lower costs while maintaining control over the service.

Because of its widespread use at the federal level, the term privatization has a number of connotations that might convince local governments not to consider alternative service delivery in order to avoid political opposition and misunderstanding. As a result communities can refrain from using these options because they fear the political reaction rather than viewing them as different methods to improve productivity and deliver services.

WHAT ALTERNATIVE SERVICE DELIVERY METHODS ARE AVAILABLE?

The following are the alternative service delivery approaches that will be discussed in this chapter.

Contracting

The local government contracts with private firms (profit and nonprofit) or another government to deliver all or a portion of a public service. The government defines the service level and quality and pays the contractor directly. This option would also include agreements whereby private firms construct and operate facilities for localities.

Many governments contract for services such as ambulance services, towing services, street construction and maintenance, or health care. The scope of contracted services is very broad; almost every local government service imaginable has been contracted in some community somewhere. Many communities also contract the construction and operation of facilities such as wastewater treatment plants, hospitals, and correctional facilities. This is most beneficial as a means of obtaining the expertise of the private company for the delivery of technical service or avoiding public debt limits imposed upon communities.

The limitations lie only in the number of available providers and the ability of the communities to define satisfactorily the service, so that it can be measured, quantified, and adequately delivered. Without competition between vendors, localities are not likely to get the cost saving that is the primary reason for using contracts. Replacing public employees with a private firm that does not have competitors is likely to be risky. Care must also be given to the description of the service in the contract. Service modifications, while possible after the initiation of the contract, may be costly. While almost any service can be defined in terms of inputs, it is more desirable to define contracts in terms of outputs. As this is not possible in all cases, communities may want to select carefully the services they consider for contracting.

Many localities might be surprised at the number and scope of contracts they are probably already using. Conducting an inventory of contracts is often a valuable tool for local officials to assess the use of this option realistically.

Franchise Concessions

The local government awards exclusive or nonexclusive rights to private firms to deliver a public service within a specific geographic region. Cable television, utilities, or towing services are examples of services in which franchises often exist. A snack bar at a park is an example of a concession. In both cases, the citizen-consumer pays the delivering firm directly for a service (rather than tax dollars paying the firm) and usually defines the level of service desired.

Franchises and concessions have more limited use than contracts because their users must be clearly identifiable, so that they can be charged for the service. Recent antitrust court rulings have also made franchises less attractive to many local officials. The level of service used by each recipient must also be measurable, so that fees can be charged accurately. The lack of competition and the longer term of the franchises can subject users to large rate increases that are not easily challenged.

Subsidies

With subsidies, local governments make financial or in-kind contributions to private organizations or individuals to encourage the delivery of public services at a reduced cost to consumers. An example of an in-kind contribution is a local government's offer of free space in a public building to a private day-care center, enabling the center to deliver child day care at a reduced cost.

Subsidies have been used for many years by communities for services where the level of service is not quantifiable, including libraries, arts, elderly services, and recreation. For example, in a community with a volunteer fire department, the community may not be able to determine the level of service needed, but the fire company can determine the cost to keep one fire truck operating. The subsidy relates to the direct cost needs rather than measurable service needs or outputs.

Often, localities do not carefully monitor how the money given to these organizations is spent or measure other service quality activities but instead make a general contribution to the organization. In many cases, there may be no competition to receive a subsidy, as one organization seeks such a grant. This could become a problem for the community if the organization's costs rise over time. However, it may still be more cost-effective than delivering the service using local employees entirely. Monitoring measures may be needed to assure that quality and productive service delivery methods are used by the organization.

Vouchers

The local government distributes vouchers (coupons or tickets with a monetary value) to citizens needing a service. Citizens select the organization from which to buy the goods or services using the voucher to offset the cost of the service partially or fully. An example is the use by senior citizens of vouchers for taxi rides. The citizen chooses a taxi company and exchanges the voucher for transportation, and the taxi company obtains reimbursement from the government.

Vouchers have limited applicability for local governments despite federal government experiments in the housing and educational areas. Vouchers work most successfully when there are multiple providers, the service is readily available, consumers have the ability and information to make a choice, and the service can be defined sufficiently, so that payment can be determined to the satisfaction of the provider and the consumer. Consumers must also be definable, so that the vouchers can be distributed to the desired group unless all citizens are to be made eligible. This has worked most successfully in local governments for paratransit services (taxis, vans), elderly services, and day care.

One drawback for local governments is that total service costs for vouchers are not as easy to control as with other alternative service options. Because consumers select the level and price of the service (possibly within guidelines established by the government), demand is hard to predict or control. Limitations on use and reimbursement levels are possible as cost-controlling measures, but vouchers may not be a cost-saving measure for localities. The desirability lies instead in the increased consumer selection over the type and level of the service.

Volunteers

Many local governments receive free help from individual citizens in delivering all or part of a public service. Most localities use these nonpaid employees to supplement the work of paid employees and to improve the quality of life in the community. Volunteers are used in many departments for many services. It is the second most used alternative service delivery method in local governments. Use includes the traditional fire departments, libraries, parks, and art facilities as well as more recently internal operations such as data processing, administration, public relations, and less traditional areas such as public works. Often the only limit to volunteer use in a community is the extent of the local government's imagination and innovation.

Like contracting, volunteers must be used as a management strategy to cut costs and improve services. This includes identifying needs, developing a program and policy, providing training where appropriate, and supervising the volunteers. Without this approach, volunteers may not be successful for local governments.

Self-Help

With self-help, local governments encourage individuals or groups, such as neighborhood groups or community organizations, to undertake or participate in an activity for their own benefit, thereby reducing the amount of government work that otherwise would be required. Self-help activities may supplement or replace local government service delivery systems. An example is the matching of carpool participants by the local government resulting in a reduced demand on public facilities.

Self-help can be used for many services, particularly if service demands increase. Self-help is usually used for services such as elderly programs, tree trimming, recreation, and crime prevention. The nationally recognized neighborhood watch program is a good example of a self-help program.

Limitations include services in which there might be danger or high risk or highly specialized services. Services that require constant attention by the same person might also not be appropriate. Neighborhood watch is successful when many different people become involved.

Incentives

When local governments exert their regulatory (deregulatory) or taxing authority, they are using incentives to encourage the delivery of public services by the private sector. For example, zoning regulations may be amended to facilitate the placement of group homes in residential areas. Or, through the use of its taxing authority, a local government may give partial property tax exemptions for homes housing free day-care assistance to other families in the neighborhood.

Incentives are the least used alternative service delivery method, in part because they are not understood or easily measured or evaluated. Local officials are still examining how they might use this option. Examples exist for the construction of facilities such as convention centers, arts facilities, day-care facilities, sport facilities, and public housing. Some communities have also used zoning requirements to get sanctions from local developers or builders such as new roads or facilities. As public-private ventures become more prevalent, the use of incentives may also increase.

WHEN SHOULD LOCAL OFFICIALS CONSIDER ALTERNATIVE SERVICE DELIVERY?

Public delivery of the vast majority of local services has become the norm in the twentieth century without regard for the type of service or the appropriateness of public delivery for these services. But are other options available? Some of these services may not exist in the private sector, so no private providers exist. Obviously, in such a case it is unlikely that there can be private delivery of the service. However, it may be possible to create such deliverers as some communities have encouraged. Former local employees have started firms, and the private sector is viewing the local government market as an expanding arena for selling services that were not available ten years ago. As a result, private deliverers exist for many services delivered presently by communities.

Consideration of alternative service delivery options is often prompted by productivity or financial problems within a local government service area. An alternative delivery option is often seen as an easy way to solve a productivity problem, reduce costs, or respond to community complaints. Some communities use the consideration of an alternative service delivery option as a means of bargaining with local employees for productivity improvements.

Before initiating any alternative service delivery option, it is useful to determine whether cost savings can be achieved through productivity improvements with local employees. In some cases, some of the cost savings that would be gained through a contract could also be gained by making policy, personnel, or equipment changes with local employees. If an alternative service delivery method cannot achieve additional savings beyond what the local government could do on its own, it may not be as attractive. However, if it meets other objectives and goals, then it may be appropriate, even if it does not result in greater savings. For example, many communities find that the cost saving from using volunteers is not easily measured, but it can meet other goals such as community involvement.

It is not fair, then, to argue that alternative service delivery options are viable in every case. Cost savings may not be great enough to justify the risks associated with change to the private contractor. Equally important, even if it were viable to contract three years ago when a contract might have been first awarded, it may not be any longer. Local governments may have been able to learn enough from the contractor about their operation to be competitive with private firms. Some experts argue that the change alone from public to private or vice versa results in productivity gains and should be done every few years. Many officials are beginning to talk about "publicization" whereby a locality returns to delivering the service in-house after a period of contracting. Evidence of this is sketchy and anecdotal at present, but it may become more prevalent in the future especially if localities can develop entrepreneurial attitudes about service delivery.

ISSUES TO BE CONSIDERED

Before committing to an alternative service delivery method, local officials may want to consider several issues. While many of these issues may be easy to address for a single service area, some communities have found it valuable to review a variety of service areas and options before beginning implementation.

It may also be useful to inventory what is already being done. For example, there may already be volunteers in schools, libraries, or hospitals; contracts may also be in use in areas not known to top officials. A look at what is being done is a starting point for an evaluation of additional uses of these approaches.

Creating a Community Vision

What mix of services does the community want? What is the acceptable level and type of services demanded by the public to meet the vision of what the community should be? What services are viewed as essentially public services in the community, and which are inherently private (this will change over time)? The recipients' ability to pay may be a determining factor in the selection of the appropriate deliverer for some services. The community vision needs to be determined by elected officials with help from staff and the public. It can easily be done as part of a budget process.

Determining the Level of Service

Local officials must also decide what the quantity and quality of services should be. For example, should trash be picked up once or twice a week? How often should streets be swept, if at all? Local officials will need to weigh the costs and potential benefits of various service levels to meet the desired community vision within the available resources. If a contract is to be used, service levels may not change from what is presently being delivered in-house, but a service level must be determined and quantified.

Determining Who Should Pay

Public services are no longer provided just using money collected through real estate, income, or sales taxes. If a service is provided to all citizens, tax revenues are most frequently used. If users or beneficiaries can be clearly identified, user fees or special assessments may be charged. Financing options may also be combined for particular services. The method of payment may influence the type of delivery option selected.

Who Can Deliver the Service

Local officials need to determine the type of providers in their community who can deliver the service. Three major options are available—using local employees, using an intergovernmental agreement, or using a private service provider (alternative service delivery approach). A combination of these approaches may also be used. If no alternative providers exist, then this option cannot be considered. If they do exist, then further steps must be taken to determine whether these providers are the best option for the community. Evaluation criteria for this assessment are discussed later in this chapter. Also, the community vision discussed earlier should describe which services the local government believes should not be provided privately. For example, some communities would not consider contracting fire services, even though private providers exist.

THE MOST SUITABLE SERVICE DELIVERY APPROACH

Five criteria can be used when determining the most appropriate service delivery approach:

• cost;
• service quality, level and effectiveness;
• impact on other local services;
• potential for service disruption;
• responsiveness to citizens' needs and expectations.

Cost

Cost is often the primary consideration in the assessment of the alternative that is most appropriate. Local officials must determine which alternative will be the most cost effective, taking care to include all costs and determine if cost savings are sufficient to risk a change in service delivery method. It is important, however, to not limit consideration to cost alone.

Service Quality, Level, and Effectiveness

No matter which service delivery method is selected, local officials continue to have the responsibility for evaluating the service quality, level, and effectiveness. The ability of any service provider to meet these expectations will ultimately help to determine the appropriateness of an alternative service delivery approach for a community.

Impact on Other Local Services

Any consideration of a change in the service delivery method should include the potential impact this change might have on the ability of the community to deliver other services. Do the same employees deliver four or five services? Is equipment shared between departments? How are emergencies handled? Often these potential problems can be resolved smoothly if identified prior to implementation of an approach.

Potential for Service Disruption

Local officials must evaluate the risk of service interruption. What would be the consequences of a day, week, or longer interruption in service if a provider were to fail to deliver the service? Interruptions in some services are less problematic than others, and the availability of substitute providers for some may decrease the problem. But if a government service monopoly is being replaced by the private service monopoly, local officials must use caution. Furthermore, how easily can the decision be reversed if service quality suffers? Can the local government easily get back into the "business"? Factors such as equipment needs, ease of hiring personnel, and start-up time required will influence this decision.

Responsiveness to Citizens' Needs and Expectations

Local governments are responsible for providing numerous services, regardless of delivery approach. Because citizens ultimately look to their local government for satisfaction, local officials cannot abdicate their service responsibilities if a provider other than the local government delivers a service. With any alternative service delivery approach, the local government has a responsibility to keep abreast of the situation and meet the changing needs and expectations of the public. Measurements of this responsiveness potential can be incorporated in contracts, franchises, and most other alternative delivery options.

Planning the Implementation of the Service Delivery Approach

How is the implementation to take place? How will the employees delivering the service be handled? Who will monitor the contract? Will a contract be phased in or all at once? These management decisions must be prepared in a plan for movement from one delivery approach to another.

Evaluating the Service on a Regular Basis

A formal or informal method of evaluating a service should be developed to determine whether the goals of elected and appointed officials and the needs of citizens are being met. For srvices delivered directly to citizens, complaints or client evaluations are the method of determining service satisfaction. For other services, local government staff needs to review the service periodically to determine whether changes are necessary. Elected officials can then use this information to determine what services should be provided and what service levels are necessary. Review and evaluation is a critical component of service delivery that cannot be overlooked, regardless of whether the service is delivered by the public or private sector.

CONCLUSION

Local officials are considering the adoption of alternative service delivery approaches for many services. While they can be a means of reducing costs, improving service quality or technical capability, and increasing community involvement, these delivery methods must be designed, managed, and evaluated in the same rigorous manner that in-house employees would be assessed. With care, these options can be a valuable tool available to management.

3

Alternative Delivery of Services in Rochester, New York

ED DOHERTY

Private contracting has become an important element in cost-cutting strategies of municipal governments. The city of Rochester, New York, has had a long experience with using private contracts for the delivery of public services. But like many communities, Rochester significantly accelerated its private contracting efforts in the late 1970s to meet mounting fiscal pressures. This discussion will explore Rochester's experience, including an analysis and description of the city's program, a review of cost and service delivery impacts, and an examination of policy control and personnel issues.

BACKGROUND

Rochester, New York's third largest city, has a resident population of 242,000 and serves as the hub for a metropolitan area of 1 million people. Like most major cities in the Northeast, Rochester faced severe decline in the 1970s. The city's population had already lost 11 percent from its 1950 peak of 332,000. The 1980 census population count reflected an additional reduction of 18 percent from 1970, for a total reduction of 17 percent since 1950. Dramatic revenue losses accompanied the population decline. A reduction in the city's assessed value cut the property tax yield by $10 million, while the distribution of the county sales tax was cut by $5 million in 1970 and an additional $6 million in 1980. The most dramatic cut, however, came in 1978, when New York State's highest court ordered a reduction of $16 million in the city's municipal property tax levy and an additional $16 million cut in the tax levy for the fiscally dependent city school district.[1] Rochester was clearly faced with an overwhelming fiscal problem. So dramatic was the city's condition that a 1976 Brookings Institution study ranked it as the sixth most distressed central city in America.[2]

In 1974 a newly elected administration undertook a multifaceted effort to rehabilitate the city. The major features of this effort were neighborhood preservation, economic development, revenue diversification, improved intergovernmental assistance, organizational restructuring, and significant cutback management. Private contracting played a major role in the city's cutback management strategy.

The city of Rochester has achieved a noteworthy record in its efforts to cut expenditures. Total operating expenditures have increased at a rate significantly below the growth in prices. In fact, if the operating budget had grown at the same level as consumer prices, the 1987-1988 budget would have been $45.4 million or 19.5 percent greater than it was. Furthermore, if these incremental expenditures were financed with the real property tax, the 1987-1988 tax levy would have been more than double its actual level.

PRIVATE CONTRACTS—A DESCRIPTION

Before 1974 Rochester used private contracts in the provision of only five basic services, other than contracts for minor support functions. These five—residential snowplowing, street lighting, volunteers for property salvage at fire scenes, ambulance service, and vehicle towing—were historical arrangements whose commencement dates cannot be accurately fixed. Over the next fourteen years, the city initiated 105 new contracts for service. In addition, "privatization" was implemented through several informal arrangements and volunteer programs. The contracts range in scope from the operation of major municipal facilities to the maintenance of small residential malls (the smallest is 0.1 acre). Of the total, fifty-eight contracts are with private firms and forty-seven are with not-for-profit agencies. The contracts can be generally divided into six groups:

1. *Entrepreneurial activities.* These consist of operating several enterprise functions (municipal parking, sports arena, convention center) and the collection of outstanding parking fines. The fourteen remaining contracts in this classification are generally based on percentages of revenue receipts, thus providing marketing incentives to the private contractors.

2. *Maintenance of neighborhood open spaces.* Thirty-one acres of neighborhood parks, 12 acres of street malls, and 600 vacant lots have been contracted to community and neighborhood groups for maintenance. The twenty-one contracts in this group are generally based on negotiated per acre rates. In the case of street malls, the neighborhoods benefit in two ways: the contracts provide cash for neighborhood

organization activities, and the net cost savings are passed along directly to the neighborhood through a reduction in the benefit assessment. In essence, the neighborhood is caring for its own facilities and assessing itself for the cost.

3. *Human services.* In implementing federally funded programs, the city decided to minimize the growth of staff by using private contractors. City staff responsibilities are generally limited to planning and administration. While this category has lessened in importance with federal program cutbacks, the city still administers seventeen contracts in this area.

4. *Specialized services.* Services of a highly technical nature have generally been converted to private contract. While these most frequently involve professional services (engineering, computer programming), trade skills (electrical, painting, roofing) have also been involved.

5. *Operational support.* The remaining contracts are for components of services that have essentially continued to be performed by city staff. In one instance (recreation center) private contracts allow comparisons with city operations. In most other cases, contracts are used to supplement city functions (grave digging, vehicles repair, janitorial services).

6. *Volunteer programs.* Though not governed by formal contracts, the city has initiated several major programs that use volunteers to supplement city efforts. The most significant areas are recreation and police, which employ volunteer coordinators. In recreation, 29,900 average annual volunteer hours were recorded over the past eight years, the equivalent of fourteen full-time employees. If valued at one-half the rate of paid staff, this program saves the city approximately $148,000 per year.

CONTRACTS HELP CONTROL COSTS

Cost control is the single most common motivation for private contracting. One author goes so far as to point out, "Perhaps the most important key to cutting costs is privatization."[3] While this point may be argued, most will agree that private contracting is an important strategy for cost control. In an evaluation of the now famous Scottsdale, Arizona, private contract for fire service, Roger S. Ahlbrandt observed, "Contracting poses two potential sources of cost savings, more efficient scale of operation and more efficient production techniques."[4]

Financially Rochester's experiences have been highly successful. Conservatively estimated, recent privatization applications are directly responsible for a $3.4 million reduction in the city's 1987-1988 operating budget.[5] The municipal property tax levy would have been 8.9 percent higher had these savings not been realized. This does not include the savings associated with private contracts in effect prior to 1974 or savings in programs where private contracting was considered but subsequently rejected.

The following summarizes Rochester's private contracting initiatives since 1974:

Program	No. of Contracts	Full Time Work Force Reduction	Annual Cost Savings
Public Works	76	267	$2,381,900
Leisure Services	4	34	575,800
Public Safety	1	14	53,000
Human Services	17	0	50,000
Administration and Finance	7	0	350,000
	105	314	$3,410,700

Private contracting savings result from several basic economic factors. Robert Poole outlines two ways in which private contracting can lead to control of public costs: The first is the elimination of public service, which can then be turned over to private forces. In these situations, the public will seek out services individually, or will collectively use contracts or volunteerism. The second way that contracting leads to cost control is through the increased efficiency that results from the private sector profit motive, the ability to achieve economies of scale, and the ability to attract and retain more skilled workers.[6]

Using Poole's model, Rochester's contracting program can be analyzed in several categories:

1. *Basic service provision.* While the city of Rochester has not abandoned any public services, it has been forced to adjust levels of service. In the case of recreation, 46 percent of the city's full-service facilities (eleven centers) have been closed during the past fifteen years, and service-hour reductions of 25 percent have been imposed at the remaining facilities. To supplement recreation and other services, several coordinated volunteer programs have been instituted.

2 *The profit motive.* The entrepreneurial activities turned over to private contractors are the most successful of Rochester's privatization efforts, accounting for savings of approximately $2.9 million. The ability of the private operators to control expenses while increasing business is the key to the savings in this group. In the municipal parking fund, an operating deficit of $1.6 million in 1975 was converted to a profit by 1984. The sports arena experienced operating deficits of approximately $300,000, which have been converted to profits of approximately $30,000, and the recently opened Convention Center is being operated by a private management corporation.

3. *Economies of scale.* Reduced unit production costs associated with scale are often difficult to measure in the service industry, both public and private. Janitorial companies who gear up to serve a large number of users provide a good example of the type of economies of scale that have benefited Rochester. A more subtle economy of scale is in the form of expertise. Rochester's contracts for municipal parking and the sports arena are with firms that operate on national and regional levels. Their ability to tap greater expertise than local operations is a type of economy of scale.

4. *More skilled employees.* Public managers are only being realistic when they recognize

government's limitations in employing individuals with specialized technical skills. Salary and civil service restrictions do not encourage direct municipal employment of such individuals. The city of Rochester has contracted for such professional services as medical, legal, engineering, and computer programming. The same principles that motivate governments to contract for professional services suggest benefits in contracting for the skilled trades. Thus, Rochester has converted to contracts for basic painting, roofing, electrical, and street resurfacing services. Savings of approximately $240,000 have been experienced through these contracts.

EVALUATING SERVICE EFFECTIVENESS

That virtually all services transferred to private contractors over the past fourteen years are still being performed on a contractual basis suggests a high degree of satisfaction with the contract arrangements. To measure service satisfaction with Rochester's private contracts, city complaint records were reviewed. Changes in recordkeeping procedures and a lack of adequate detail in the records limit the conclusions that can be drawn. However, the review of complaints does indicate that there were no significant increases in citizen complaints during the period when contracts were being introduced. In fact, in the early years of expanded contracting (1975-1979), complaints showed a steady decline. Several years of stability followed (1979-1981), then came three years (1982-1984) of gradual increases and further stability (1985-1987).[7]

Several formal evaluations of Rochester's service contracts have been undertaken, and they further demonstrate that private contractors are performing effectively. One such evaluation concluded that "the Clinton-Baden recreation program was substantially meeting contractual performance and participation objectives."[8] A review of private contracts for the maintenance of vacant lots was very direct in its positive findings: "It is concluded that private contracting through the Adopt-A-Lot Program is 73% more efficient (as measured in dollars) and 22% more effective (in rated appearance) than traditional City maintenance."[9]

As described previously, many of Rochester's contracted activities involved enterprise activities. Improved customer use of these facilities may be considered an indication of satisfaction. In fact, many economists would suggest that a customer's willingness to purchase a service at a given price and under given conditions is the only true measure of satisfaction. Rochester's experience with leasing municipal parking facilities provides a good illustraiton of this principle. After commencing its lease of the downtown parking ramps, the private operator began to reduce costs by limiting the number of exit cashiers. This in turn increased the public's waiting time. While there were a number of complaints, the city continued the contract, the operator continued the practice, and the public continued to patronize the garages. The lesson of this anecdote is that political decision making would not—as it hadn't in the many years of direct city operations—tolerate the service reduction inherent in longer lines. The private contractor, with extensive experience elsewhere, was able to gauge accurately the necessary staffing patterns that would assure continued customer support. Use of the city's parking facilities has increased steadily over the past ten years, as had attendance at the city's sports arena, which was also leased.

Unfortunately, most municipal services are not directly susceptible to market mechanisms. Public safety, sanitation, snow plowing, and street maintenance bear too directly on the common welfare to have service levels determined on the basis of demand responses of groups of individuals. An incident in the late winter of 1984 caused significant alarm for the Rochester city administration and raised serious questions about one of the city's oldest applications of private contracting. Rochester is well known for its heavy snowfall. In late February to early March, the city experienced its second worst snow storm in history (34.5 inches in three days). As has been standard operation for many years, private contractors were dispatched to clear the city's residential streets. Significant contractor failure left several neighborhoods buried for days after the storm. The incident was probably Rochester's greatest service breakdown in ten years and led influential City Councilman Paul E. Haney to state, "I'm going to demand some answers and look into the whole contract system."[10]

Beyond its impact on Rochester, this incident illustrates an area of weakness for the application of private contracting—emergency response. In emergencies, the public has traditionally turned to government, which is expected to respond regardless of cost. This simply cannot be expected of private companies. In fact, basic market mechanisms may work counter to public interest during emergencies. In the case of snow removal, a contractor will bid a rate prior to the snow season, but the market rates will escalate dramatically after a foot of snow has fallen, thus providing a strong incentive to ignore the public contract. The local government can require performance bonds and penalties to protect against this situation, but, of course, these provisions drive up the cost of service. Rochester's plan in response to the 1984 problems called for tightening contract specifications, strengthening contractor inspection, and providing some municipal backup to the contractors, but the basic private contractor arrangement continued.

POLICY CONTROL

Policy control is another important issue for municipalities considering the use of private contracting. Rochester has certainly experienced some of the problems associated with relinquishing of control:

• The operator of the city's stadium (now closed) had arranged for an exhibition game between a local rugby team and a team from South Africa. A stream of protest over South Africa's racial policies was directed at City Hall, but the city's contract gave it no control over who played at the facility.

• Soon after entering into a lease for the operation of its sports arena, the city of Rochester received significant pressure because the regional high school basketball championship tournament was threatened with eviction from the facility. The popular annual event could not pay the rates being charged by the new operator, and the city's lease carried no provision for subsidized events.

Both incidents were settled through negotiations with the contractors, but they serve to illustrate the range of potential problems.

In other cases, Rochester was more successful in retaining policy control. In its lease of downtown parking facilities, the city very carefully preserved its control over parking rates. In doing so, the administration reserved maximum flexibility in using municipal parking as an economic development tool. Of course, a cost was incurred. Without rate control, the prospective operators could not be certain of the revenue potential from the system. Therefore, they were likely to be conservative in their bids. The percentage return to the city increased with each contract rebidding, indicating that as the contractors gained confidence in the city's willingness to increase parking rates, they became willing to improve their bids. If changes in parking volume and expenses could be controlled, it would be possible to quantify the cost to the city for retaining control.

Perhaps the key to the control issue lies in the separation of government's roles as producer and arranger of services. As discussed by E. S. Savas, this separation allows government to discontinue its production role, but retain control through its arranger role.[11] As Rochester's experience demonstrates, local communities must be willing to face some loss of oversight to realize the full economic benefits of private contracting, though it is possible to retain important elements of control. Thus, major private contracting operations call for a balancing of opportunity and risk.

PERSONNEL ISSUES

Personnel concerns, particularly labor-management issues, require careful consideration. There are wide variations in labor law from state to state. In turn, management discretion in initiating private contracts also varies. The critical interpretation is in "drawing the line when a topic is at one and the same time a term or condition of employment, or directly affects terms and conditions, and also relates to basic public policy considerations that fall within the category of management prerogative."[12] In states like New York, which have strong labor legislation, private contracting applications may be seriously restricted. New York State's Public Employee Relations Board (PERB) has tended to interpret private contracts as subcontracting, with the prime contract being the labor agreement. "If the employer's objective in subcontracting is solely economic, that is to reduce cost without intent to alter the character of the services provided the public in any significant way, the general rule is that the matter is a mandatory subject and the decision must be negotiated."[13] The basis for such PERB rulings is that subcontracting results in the reassignment of unit work to nonbargaining unit employees, in violation of New York's Taylor Law.

Rochester has been fortunate to be able to implement its private contracts despite New York's restrictive statutes. In part, the city's effectiveness can be attributed to a lack of experience on the part of its unions in dealing with private contracting during the early stages. More recently, however, the unions have become more sensitive to the issue.[14] Recent consideration of expanding the city's janitorial contract was put aside in the face of union objections.

While labor laws provide real limitations on a government's discretion to use private contracts, there are still opportunities:

- Management prerogatives are still widely recognized. When reorganizing or restructuring service delivery mechanisms, considerable latitude remains to implement private contracts.

- Responses to new service demands are usually not subject to existing labor contracts, and therefore, should be considered as prime applications for private contracting. When Rochester opened its new Convention Center in 1985, it immediately pursued a private contracting arrangement, thus avoiding any labor-management dispute.

- Negotiations may well prove fruitful, particularly if the alternative to private contracting is perceived to be work force reductions and layoffs. Restrictions on layoffs or guarantees of preference in private contract hiring are techniques which may ease the negotiations.

In addition to labor relations, there are other personnel issues that should be considered in managing the change brought about by private contracting. Employee morale is likely to be adversely affected if change is very dramatic or is perceived as unnecessary, or if no consideration is extended to affected employees.[15] Rochester was able to implement its work-force reductions over an extended time frame, thus minimizing disruption. There were layoffs, but they were minimized by efforts to place workers in other city agencies or with the private contractors. The city's agreements with contractors required that interviews and consideration be given to displaced city workers. Perhaps the greatest aid in maintaining morale was the fact that the city's financial plight was well known and generally accepted by employees as fact. In addition, efforts to secure additional funding for city programs were made and were well publicized. Furthermore, many of the most significant changes in Rochester took place during the near-default of New York City. This timing provided a sort of external justification of Rochester's actions.

PRIVATE CONTRACTS NOT ALWAYS USED

The benefits of private contracting are often realized even when contracts are not implemented. The scrutiny and analysis required in the consideration of private contracting often facilitate improvements even when public service delivery continues. Management expert John Diebold points out, "even if we continue to keep most services in the public sector, we could do a much better job and cut costs if we used technology more aggressively and more imaginatively."[16] Rochester's experience with its solid waste collection and disposal services illustrates this point well. In 1974-1975, the city of Rochester spent $8.6 million for refuse collection and disposal. If this service had not been dramatically overhauled, price increases would have driven the costs to a 1987-1988 level of $18.6 million. However, the 1987-1988 budget calls for refuse expenditures of only $11.6 million, a real savings of $7 million. Additionally, the current budget is fully loaded, including a reserve for equipment replacement, and is financed through a separate user charge. The 1974-1975 program covered only the costs of direct operations and was fully financed through property tax and other local revenues. Obviously, major service changes were required to accomplish these benefits, and private contracting played an important role.

Faced with a service that was recognizably inefficient, Rochester considered the use of private contractors. In 1976 bids were actually received for a contract to cover refuse collection in the northwest quadrant of the city. While the bids indicated a significant potential for savings, concerns over service guarantees, displaced employees, and surplus equipment led the city to pause before making a final decision. This pause proved fortuitous, as the city's union, American Federation of State, County and Municipal Employees (AFSCME), Local 1635, decided that an offer to save union jobs would be in order. That offer called for the reduction in crew size from four to three persons per truck throughout the city. The savings from this offer exceeded those of the private contract, so the city agreed. In this instance, the private-contract option provided the incentive needed for efficiencies in a municipally operated program. Subsequent technological improvements allowed for further crew size and route reductions, producing additional savings.[17]

CONCLUSION

Private contracting has served Rochester well. It has not been a panacea, nor has it been implemented without difficulty. However, the city's efforts in private contracting have produced clear cost savings, allowed for continued quality in service delivery, and maintained an acceptable level of public policy control.

NOTES

1. *Waldert v. City of Rochester*, 44 N.Y. 2d 831 (1978). In this case, the court ruled that property taxes for retirement and social security expenses were subject to New York's constitutional real property tax limit. Consistent with state legislation, the city of

Rochester (and other cities) had levied property taxes in excess of its limit to finance these costs.

2. Richard P. Nathan and Charles Adams, "Understanding Central City Hardship," Technical Services Reprint No. T-012 (Washington, DC: Brookings Institution, 1976).

3. Robert W. Poole, Jr., *Cutting Back City Hall* (New York: Universe Books, 1980), p. 26.

4. Robert S. Ahlbrandt, Jr., "Implications of Contracting for Public Service," *Urban Affairs Quarterly* 9, no. 3 (March 1974): 339.

5. Cost savings were determined by comparing precontract staffing levels and current salary schedules with actual current costs. Volunteers were valued at one-half city staff, except in the case of uniformed positions, in which case a one-third value was used.

6. Poole, *Cutting Back City Hall*, p. 27.

7. City of Rochester, *Annual Reports*, 1974-1975 through 1977-1978. City of Rochester, Monthly Service Office Complaint Summary, July 1978 through June 1987.

8. City of Rochester, "Evaluation of Baden Street Recreation Program Contract Operation," Bureau of Budget and Efficiency Report, September 16, 1985.

9. City of Rochester, "Adopt-a-Lot Evaluation," Bureau of Budget and Efficiency Report, April 7, 1986.

10. *Rochester Democrat and Chronicle*, March 1, 1984, p. 4A.

11. E. S. Savas, *Privatizing the Public Sector* (Chatham, NJ: Chatham House, 1982).

12. Ronald Donovan and Marsha J. Orr, *Subcontracting in the Public Sector: The New York Experience*. Institute of Public Management Monograph No. 10 (Ithaca, NY: New York School of Industrial and Labor Relations at Cornell University, 1982), p. 19.

13. Ibid., p. 22.

14. Note the "It Looks Good on Paper, But" advertising by the American Federation of State, County and Municipal Employees (AFSCME).

15. Larry Hirschhorn, *Cutting Back: Retrenchment and Redevelopment in Human and Community Services* (San Francisco: Jossey-Bass, 1983).

16. "Ways Private Firms Can Save Money for Burdened Cities: Money-Short Cities Can Cut Costs, Operate More Efficiently, by Letting Private Companies Compete in Providing Basic Services," an interview with John Diebold, *U.S. News and World Report*, November 17, 1975.

17. "Bold City Management Cuts Collection Costs," *Waste Age*, December 1980, and Peter Korn and James E. Malone, "We Cut Collection Costs, Not Service," *American City and County*, March 1981.

4

Florence, Kentucky, Adapts to Growth

BRUCE JANKEN AND BETSY CONRAD

This chapter contains three "historical" topics and a brief reflection and glimpse into the future. First is a description of the city, with emphasis on its unusual growth and large nearby cities. These unusual characteristics encouraged Florence to continue to develop and refine agreements with government neighbors that had experience delivering safety, recreational, data processing, and other services in the public sector. The second part of the chapter describes these programs. The third topic is services provided by agreements with private companies, which currently include waste collection, janitorial, construction, and towing services.

BRIEF DESCRIPTION OF A HIGH-GROWTH CITY

The city of Florence is one of the fastest growing cities in Kentucky. Located in Boone County, the city is home to nearly 20,000 residents and host to probably 100,000 people daily, as it is a vital regional commercial center. The city is bisected by the heavily traveled Interstate 71/75 and is adjacent to the Greater Cincinnati International Airport. One of the area's largest industrial parks is situated on the city's southern border, where railway access is available to augment the interstate and airport transportation facilities.

Relationship to Metro Area and the Commonwealth

As part of the Greater Cincinnati area, Boone County, along with the other northern-most Kentucky counties of Kenton and Campbell, has historically experienced what has been called a "step-child" relationship with the Commonwealth of Kentucky. Many of the residents worked in downtown Cincinnati or in the urban centers of Covington and Newport on the Kentucky side of the river. The economic ties to Cincinnati seemed more binding than the legislative connections to Frankfort. The multitude of small political jurisdictions in northern Kentucky contributed to the inability of the three-county area to form a substantial power base in spite of the population concentration.

Brief History of Development

Until the post–World War II housing boom brought rapid subdivision development to northern Kentucky, Florence was a small rural town on the Dixie Highway with little commercial activity other than a gas station, a couple of restaurants, a drug store, and a sprinkling of tourist homes on the outskirts. The city's population explosion during the 1950s brought the common rapid-growth problems of school overcrowding, water shortage, sewage pollution from more septic tanks than the soil could accommodate, and lack of adequate fire protection.

In an effort to attract industrial development, the City Council offered revenue bonds to corporations seeking to build new plants on relatively inexpensive real estate with reasonably adequate infrastructure and availability of a rather cheap labor pool. Many of these companies were relocating from Cincinnati's deteriorating and crowded inner city.

During the late 1950s and early 1960s, the construction of the interstate highway system and the conversion of hundreds of acres of pastureland south of the city into a modern light industrial park brought another surge of development activity.

Even though attracting this development was a major goal of the city leaders, they had difficulty meeting the heavy demands for services. The municipal sewer system was in its infancy, there was a shortage of water, and many of the roadways leading off the main thoroughfares were still unpaved.

The decade of the 1970s brought rapid commercial development to the area with the construction of the tri-state area's largest indoor shopping mall and the numerous subordinate developments. The demand for housing was exceeding the supply, and market-wise developers began construction of numerous apartment complexes. The fairly liberal zoning regulations allowed duplexes and some larger apartment buildings in what had been exclusively single-family residential subdivisions. Soon the townspeople were alarmed over the influx of what they considered to be a less stable population group and implored the city officials to limit such development. But the demands of the market spoke louder than all the complaints of the citizenry. It was as though the once sought-after development had somehow gotten out of control, and the city fathers felt they had little power to slow down this steamroller which was gobbling up the city, especially as commercial growth began encroaching upon their homes.

AGREEMENTS WITH OTHER PUBLIC AND QUASI-PUBLIC AGENCIES

Fire Services

As in thousands of other small rural communities across America, fire fighting in Florence was accomplished with volunteers on the bucket brigade. A large fire cistern was constructed under Main Street to provide a source of water to fight the occasional fires in the town's structures, most of which were built of wood. When there weren't enough local townsfolk to fight a fire, a frantic call went out to the organized volunteer department in neighboring Elsmere, and the town trustees were billed for the services.

In 1937, a group of local citizens formally organized Florence Volunteer Fire Department, Inc. A used truck was purchased with town funds, but the group operated on contributions collected from property owners. A Ladies Auxiliary was formed to assist with fund-raising projects. The truck was kept in a garage in the rear of a gas station on Main Street. Ten years later, the city constructed a combination fire house-community center on Main Street with the financial help of some generous citizens.

The fire department's service area included territory well beyond the town boundaries, including the industrial park. Although the park occupants had received industrial revenue bond financing through the city, Florence council had been reluctant to push the issue of annexation. It seemed unnecessary for property tax base purposes at that time anyway, since the bonding agreements had relieved these firms from the burden of taxation during the twenty-year life of the bond program!

The effect of the area's rapid development on the fire department was obvious. Even though the city continued to provide financing for major equipment and apparatus purchases, the fund-raising campaigns were not sufficiently successful to support the increased operational needs. In 1967, the city council agreed to contract with the Florence Volunteer Fire Department for fire protection services to the areas within the corporate boundaries. The amount of the contract was determined by a calculation involving the annual property valuation total. In 1971, the annual contract amount was $21,349, and by 1987, the total came to $382,170.

A billing system was implemented, and subsequently a taxing district was created to raise revenue from service areas outside corporate boundaries. The occupants of the industrial park contracted individually with the fire department for services. Property for a second fire station in the industrial park was donated by the Industrial Park Foundation, and the building was paid for from the fire department's general fund.

Florence had the traditional problem of lack of personnel during daytime hours when most of the volunteers are at work. In 1974 the organization hired its first professional fire fighters to insure adequate protection to the community. The organization was firmly entrenched in the concept of voluntarism and continued to rely heavily on the volunteers in both line and staff positions. In 1988 there were fifteen paid members and well over forty volunteers.

Even though the fire fighters were not city employees, an agreement was reached to offer them a retirement program through the local Policemen's Pension Fund. This plan was established in 1970 and received funding from a special property tax as well as employee contributions through payroll deduction.

The Kentucky Legislature passed a bill effective in 1988 that closed existing municipal pension funds (many of which were underfunded) to new members. The new law required all newly hired hazardous duty employees of a municipality to participate in the state retirement program and required the employees already in an existing local program to decide whether to participate in the state program or remain in the local one. The state fund stipulates that participants must be employees of a municipality and cannot be employees of a separate, though nonprofit, organization. Consequently, the fire fighters requested and the City Council approved and accepted the fire department as a department of the city organization, so that their fifteen professional fire fighters could qualify to participate in the state pension fund. This was a peculiar turn-around for this organization's membership, which had, at times, considered the relationship with the city as somewhat adversarial and viewed with suspicion the city's requests for copies of financial documents.

Planning and Zoning Enforcement Services

The Florence Board of Trustees created a town planning commission in 1949; however, the first organizational meeting was not held until 1951, and the first planning and zoning ordinance was not approved until two years later. The Master Plan was created to control future growth not only within the incorporated area, but also in a five-mile surrounding radius. During the 1950s the commission reviewed and approved the steady stream of subdivision plans submitted for their consideration and recommendation to the City Council.

In 1966 the state passed legislation requiring the establishment of an area-wide planning and zoning unit. Florence was allotted six appointments to the fifteen-member panel and the cost of operating the commission was apportioned between the participating jurisdictions, namely the county government and the other two municipal corporations in the county. In 1970 the city's contribution to the commission was $3,600; by 1988 the amount had grown to $85,850.

In 1968 office space was established for the Planning Commission in the Florence Municipal Building and a part-time clerk and zoning enforcement officer were hired. As the volume of development in all sections of the county increased dramatically during the early 1980s, a planning director was added. Gradually the staff grew to include several planners and clerks, and the office moved to more spacious quarters in the new County Building.

In spite of this staffing increase, the low-paying positions attracted college-educated but inexperienced planners and the high rate of turnover made continuity of work difficult. It was necessary to hire private consulting firms to conduct the necessary research for some of the larger projects being proposed. For example, in 1983 the Planning Commission engaged a private engineering firm to conduct a special land use study of the area surrounding the nearly completed I-75 and Turfway Road Interchange, the city's new "front door." By 1988, however, the expertise of the Planning Commission staff had significantly improved, and the agency received a "Highest Honors Award" from the Kentucky Chapter of the American Planning Association for the Houston-Donaldson Land Use Study.

The Planning Commission, according to Kentucky law, is a recommending body, with the power of legislative action held by the appropriate city or county government. There are, however, certain restrictions placed on the cities and counties with regard to turning down a Planning Commission recommendation. Thus, the commission has considerable though indirect power, and the cities are precluded from acting arbitrarily.

The only formal input that the local government body can contribute during the commission's consideration of a development proposal must be made during the public hearing process. If this opportunity is missed, communication between elected and appointed officials is hampered, and any philosophical differences between the two organizations may be embarrassingly obvious.

On several occasions, members of council took exception to the recommendations made by the Planning Commission with regard to specific proposals. These instances brought forth the standard arguments from some corners that the community suffers when direct control is relinquished to a regional or centralized authority. The benefits of an area-wide planning commission are regionalized continuity of planning, coordination of effort, and the cost effectiveness of sharing a professional planning staff.

Parks and Recreation Services

Lincoln Woods, a twenty-acre park in a residential district, was developed enthusiastically during the late 1970s. The City Parks Board was created to oversee the city's first experience with a recreational facility, and the concept of county participation in the program was successfully initiated. In 1979, the county agreed to install lights at the park contingent upon the city's willingness to pay the electric bill. Unfortunately, the shelter house, restroom facilities, and playground equipment were soon vandalized, and the cost of maintenance for the park area seemed to diminish the original interest.

By 1988, the city had acquired a fifteen-acre estate, which was quickly dubbed the "nature park" because the property lends itself to passive recreation. The receipt of federal funding for development was contingent upon the city's commitment to preserving the land forever as a park.

The county was asked to participate at a greater level with the operation and maintenance of the growing city park system, and the fiscal court was persuaded to provide some assistance. The argument advanced to achieve this cooperation was that the city property owners pay county property taxes in addition to the city tax, but nearly all the services rendered to these citizens were provided by the city.

Animal Control/Shelter Services

One of the few county-funded services available to city residents is the animal control service. As this rather small department received more funding from fiscal court, the level of service improved. Additional employees were hired and the facilities and equipment were upgraded.

In an effort to contribute to the spirit of cooperation between the various city and county departments, the city agreed to the animal control service's request to sell dog tags at the municipal office for the convenience of the local residents. The animal control officer visits the city building periodically to retrieve the tag fees collected and supply the office with the necessary forms and tags. This increased contact and communication has resulted in more responsive service to the city by the animal control workers.

Public Safety Communication Services

The city and county each had separate emergency dispatching and records systems through 1979, but then an interlocal agreement was negotiated creating the Boone County Public Safety Communications Center (P.S.C.C.). Boone Center serves four law enforcement agencies, nine fire departments, and various other support agencies. Such a facility requires expensive equipment and highly trained personnel. The purpose of this consolidation was to eliminate duplication, improve interagency communication, and use resources more efficiently.

The center is jointly funded by the participating jurisdictions based on population. The original agreement called for an administrative board consisting of the county sheriff, chiefs of the county and city police departments, and representatives from the county fiscal court and the city council. The board was given direct responsibility for the conduct of the personnel and the operation of the center.

A director was hired from outside the participating organization; however, city and county dispatchers were detailed by their respective chiefs to work under the direction of the new agency head. In time, these workers became employees of the P.S.C.C., which in itself alleviated some organizational divisiveness. The primary problem, however, seemed to be the fact that the board, which was made up of persons of department-head level, the same as the P.S.C.C. director, took a hands-on approach to managing the operations of the department as well as establishing policy. Subsequently the agreement was amended to alter the makeup and duties of the board.

The original consolidation agreement also called for a merged felony squad to be created from the participating police agencies. A supervisor from one of the departments was named as director of this special unit. This arrangement failed to meet the goals and objectives set out for such a unit and after a brief time, the agreement was amended, eliminating the joint felony squad. The problems stemmed from the fact that the officers assigned to that unit were never made employees of a separate agency, but were simply detailed to the squad, and they understandably maintained loyalties to their own departments. Unfortunately this worked to the detriment of the unit and the discontinuation in the cooperative experiment.

Data Processing Services

In 1980 the city's payroll worksheets were transported by a courier service to a computer service firm for computation and check preparation. The growing number of employees and the increasingly complex deduction list made manual check calculation too time-consuming and prone to errors. Likewise, the monthly budgetary accounting information was transmitted to the city's accounting firm for transformation into a monthly report for council. The city of Covington handled data processing for the new payroll tax accounting. The annual property tax bills were processed and prepared by a computer service firm located in Lexington. Remaining accounting tasks accomplished in-house were performed manually.

In 1983 the city reviewed this situation in light of ever-expanding technology. Bids were received for the purchase of a complete computer system, and as an alternative, consideration was given to contracting with the county for time on their existing mainframe, using the government accounting software they had purchased. After evaluating the options, council agreed to purchase two terminals, which would be linked to the mainframe via microwave, and pay the monthly service fee to the county.

For many employees, this was the first experience with computers. Unlike many private sector vendors, the county could not provide more than a minimal training program for the operators. Then other local agencies followed the lead to computers, and before long, lengthy delays and time lags became the rule rather than the exception. The mainframe was upgraded to handle the growing number of users, but this improvement was short-lived. The limitations of the county computer staff contributed to that department's inability to keep the customers happy, and what had begun as an exercise in cooperation ended as a workout in frustration for both parties.

By 1987 the city was ready to step up to an in-house system with a network of personal computers. The experience of working with the county's computer system was valuable in spite of the problems. It prepared the staff members to evaluate the proposals received from vendors more effectively and made them aware of features they could require in both hardware and software to perform their tasks better.

AGREEMENTS/CONTRACTS WITH PRIVATE SECTOR ORGANIZATIONS

Solid Waste Collection

Before the era of exclusive franchise grants, several private firms collected refuse from households and businesses in the community. Large, noisy garbage trucks often lumbered down city streets in the wee hours of the morning, to the irritation of residents, or while school children waited for buses. In an effort to reduce the risk to public safety and control times of collections, the franchise concept was developed. Bids from the various waste collection firms are received and evaluated, resulting in granting an exclusive franchise for a period of two years, with optional two-year extensions built into the bidding structure.

Janitorial and Uniform Services

For many years, city employees had been responsible for keeping their own office areas clean. Public works employees were assigned to janitorial duties particularly in common areas, but these tasks were often given less priority than assignments outside City Hall. The building and contents were simply not kept clean.

A cost analysis was performed, and it was determined that the cost of hiring a professional janitorial service would be no more than hiring a full-time employee to do the job, especially when the cost of employee benefits was calculated. Bids were received for the job from several janitorial firms, and a contract was awarded. Again, the service was not up to expectations. After a period of time, the bidding process was repeated, and the contract was awarded to a different firm. A service to provide clean uniforms for public works employees was also put out to bid.

Street Construction/Resurfacing Projects

Major public works improvements are occasionally tackled by the city. These projects obviously require more personnel and equipment than are available through the city's public works department. Since these projects are not attempted frequently in a city like Florence, they are contracted with private construction firms. Oversight of these projects is provided by the city's public works director.

Towing Services

One of the areas in which the privatization concept creates revenue for the city is the towing and impound lot. If a car must be impounded, a wrecker is called from a rotating list of towing services located in the city. The car is towed to the city impound lot, and the towing service bills the city. When the owner comes to retrieve the vehicle, he or she is required not only to reimburse the city for the towing fee but also a processing fee plus daily storage charge.

The alternatives to this method are for a city to operate a tow truck, which would require not only a considerable capital outlay, but also personnel to operate it day and night, or to allow the local towing companies to provide the storage lots and claim the fees. Of course the cost involved, other than some clerical tasks, would be one-time investment of pavement and fencing, and the cost of assuming responsibility for the vehicles in storage.

REFLECTIONS AND THE FUTURE

Looking back, we see contracting and consolidation (sharing) as ways to be more efficient. Experienced producers with strong incentive save capacity costs of personnel and facilities. Consolidation also reduces capacity costs by more fully using personnel and equipment shared by two or more governments. On the downside there is some loss of control. Schedules and priorities in general must be more flexible.

The future is likely to see Florence respond more to cost pressures than to the desire for closer control of services. Building maintenance could go private. We are embarking on the development of acquired acreage for commercial and governmental use; the latter may include a library and public health services. This development will probably be managed by either the city of Covington's economic development office or by a private developer. We will probably see consolidation of law enforcement by Florence, Walton, the Boone County sheriff, and the separate county police. This sharing will save money as well as increase effectiveness. As our growth and neighbor environment evolve, we will adapt.

PART TWO

EXPERIENCES OF ALTERNATIVE DELIVERERS

5

Business Perspective—
Environmental Infrastructure

PHILIP D. GIANTRIS

Effective management of the environmental infrastructure of a society is critical, as life support, to the very existence of that society. The issues of adequate, safe water supply, and effective, sanitary wastewater treatment and disposal have challenged humankind throughout time.

The lack of environmental infrastructure seriously limits the types of land uses and population densities that we have come to accept in an industrialized society. Yet, today's problems of environmental infrastructure are not merely the lack of facilities but rather are compounded by existing facilities that are inadequate or below performance standards, or both.

It is this double-edged need of capital facilities and standards based on performance that must be addressed today. The challenge comes at a time of continuing public interest in more stringent regulatory standards and enforcement at the federal government level, while capital financing is being shifted to the state and local level in the wake of federal grant program cutbacks. This shift as seen from the local perspective only compounds the demand for limited sources of financial resources brought about by various spending and bond capacity ceilings.

In this socioeconomic climate the privatization alternative must be given serious consideration by public sector decision makers. In so doing, privatization of environmental infrastructure must be viewed at the outset as a public-private partnership toward a common objective. It is neither a *failure* of the public sector nor a *takeover* by the private sector.

Definitions are needed before going on to public and private sector perspectives. With *full service privatization* the privatizer assumes a direct responsibility to arrange for the overall project financing, provide capital equipment, and/or facilities necessary to produce the service (e.g., a treatment plant, processing facility, collection vehicles, etc.), and provide a trained workforce to operate and maintain these facilities based on agreed performance standards. This service normally would include all consumables required to meet the performance standards.

With a *contract operations and maintenance* agreement the privatizer assumes direct responsibility to provide a trained workforce to operate and maintain existing facilities or equipment normally owned by the community. This service provides for guarantees based on agreed performance standards. This service normally would include all consumables required to meet performance standards.

PUBLIC SECTOR VIEW

The public sector, manifest in those elected and appointed officials who are charged with safeguarding the public interest, has very specific and reasonable concerns when it considers privatization or contract operation of environmental infrastructure services. This is more complicated when the governmental entity has a history of building, owning, and operating its own facilities. Although the list of concerns is long, there are three that consistently rise to the top in any discussion. These are public responsibility, governmental control, and responsiveness to public concerns.

Public Responsibility

In the area of essential services such as environmental infrastructure, public officials feel an added weight of responsibility, which usually reduces itself to the decision, "We will do it ourselves." This behavior has not only been an impediment to privatization but also to more recent efforts to regionalize environmental infrastructure solutions among different governmental jurisdictions.

The public official is correct in addressing this serious responsibility, but it must be addressed in a two-step process. This process, described by E. S. Savas (1982) makes an essential split between the "provide" decision and the "produce" decision. Many public officials, having made the decision that an essential service should be provided to their constituency, automatically conclude that it should or must produce it to fulfill its responsibility.

Governmental Control

The issue of governmental control, though somewhat related to public responsibility, is more a problem of the lack of management sophistication to contractually delegate or assign tasks and activities contractually. The feeling is that if the governmental unit does not do it with its own employees, then it has lost control, that governmental employees will react directly to the wishes of the public officials whereas a private producer of services has no motivation to do so.

Responsiveness to Public Concern

The assumption by the public sector is that the private service producer has no interest in the public's concern for services. The general feeling is that the private producer of services just does the job and nothing more. The expectation is that there should be something more.

The public official needs to be comfortable with privatization and contract operations during periods of emergency and unexpected or unusual conditions. It is not the everyday, business-as-usual activities that can be readily defined; rather, it is the major flood, the drought, the pipe failure, the pressure loss, and other unpredictable events that cause public officials to question the private producer's level of public concern.

PRIVATE SECTOR VIEW

The private sector is that part of our economic society that focuses on the delivery of a product or a service based upon the concept of a profit objective as the reward for investment and risk. Classically, the private sector assesses market needs, required resources to produce, pricing options, competition, and business risk. Based on these considerations, it determines whether it can profitably participate in a market.

Essentially this same assessment has been made by the private sector in approaching the environmental infrastructure market. In making the decision to go forward, the private sector feels strongly about three specific features unique to engaging a private sector management alternative. These features are efficiency of performance, contractual accountability, and incentives to perform.

Efficiency of Performance

An established privatizer in the environmental infrastructure market has inherent efficiencies in producing services. The effect of this is that savings can be realized by the private sector that are not normally available to the public sector. The depth of technical expertise is a luxury that the public sector producer of services does not have and would need to procure individually, at a premium, to be on equal footing with the private sector. The opportunity to obtain discounts as a bulk purchaser of supplies, such as chemicals and repair and replacement parts, for multiple locations can create an economic advantage. There are other areas such as labor management, turnkey construction, and technology investment that all can result in a greater overall efficiency

Private sector firms in the environmental infrastructure market view their involvement as a business commitment with a focused desire to be in that business. For the private sector firm, wastewater management is not the necessary evil of public administration, but rather an exciting, opportunity market.

Control Accountability

Contractors in the private sector are accustomed to contractual relationships that set standards of performance and bases for compensation. When a privatizer agrees to construct or operate a wastewater treatment facility for a public entity, both the company and the public entity know what is expected and what the penalties are for nonperformance. Structured correctly, in a privatization situation, the public entity has actually increased rather than decreased its control over a functional area of critical services. Generally, there is a no basis for similar control or contractual accountability with a public employee staff.

This accountability is built around a service contract. James C. Dobbs (1985) defines the service contract as

the centerpiece of the privatization transaction. The agreement provides for the terms and conditions of payment by the service recipient, and the terms of any escalation of those payments. In turn, the agreement provides for the quantity and quality of service by the service provider and specifies its performance obligations. An important function of the service contract is to allocate the risk among the parties and to provide adequate assurances that the cost of foreseeable contingencies will be funded to enhance the financial viability and credit worthiness of the project. Finally, the service contract includes the purchase option and ground rules for negotiating an extension of the service relationship if the option is not exercised.

Additional major issues to be addressed in such a contract include force majeure, changes in law, additions and modifications to projects, equipment replacement fund, and responsibility for fines and penalties.

Incentives to Perform

The private sector, both as a firm and as individual employees within the firm, normally has and offers incentives for performance that are rare to nonexistent in the public sector. It is common within the private sector to give productivity or cost savings incentives in the form of salary increases, bonuses, or promotions. In turn, the firm as a whole has an incentive as a normal part of the service contract to share in cost savings and to justify a contract renewal. In addition, as an ongoing business, the private-sector firm works to establish a reputation in a market, which is fundamentally based on prior performance and reputation. The concepts of client satisfaction and reputation are not commonly concerns of a public sector work force, which essentially functions in a monopoly environment.

CHANGING CONCEPTS OF RISK ALLOCATION
AND MANAGEMENT

Today more than ever public decision makers, whether elected or appointed officials, address the issues of capital programs and service delivery from a risk allocation and risk management standpoint. This is not meant to imply that these public decision makers did not manage risks in the past. Rather, it speaks to the increasing range of services and complexities that have become the concern of the public decision maker. Local governments receive demands from federal and state governments through legislation and regulation, and the demands from their constituencies for expanded services and cost-effective, efficient, and timely performance.

With each action undertaken at the local government level, there are associated risks. For privatization to work, according to Goldman and Mokuvos (1984, p. 58) "the proper attitude of the public/private partners is to seek to work together to:

• Identify the risks which must be addressed;
• Identify the consequences of those risks;
• Take prudent management steps to minimize the probability of the consequences occurring;
• Agree on actions to reduce and to allocate the risks, including allocation to third parties such as insurance companies."

Where capital financing is a major element of the service delivery, risk that is perceived by equity investors or potential bond buyers as not being managed or loosely allocated will result in a higher cost of capital (interest rate) and a resulting higher user fee to meet the debt service requirements.

Relative to a specific public service such as wastewater treatment the local government must be prepared to:

• commit to defined minimum usage (minimum flow)
• commit to a long-term usage
• guarantee an adequate rate structure for its users to insure sufficient revenues
• improve local use ordinances such as sewer use and industrial pretreatment

In turn, the private sector service producer must be prepared to:

• guarantee on-time completion of the needed facilities for an agreed construction price
• guarantee on-time startup and successful ongoing operation meeting all applicable regulatory standards

To be successful for both the public and private partner, each of these issues must be negotiated in the cooperative spirit of a public-private partnership. Where there has been no prior experience in the local unit of government, the concept initially seems like a road fraught with danger. But once traveled, it opens tremendous new vistas to the public decision maker in the ability to responsibly address local needs.

CHANGING CONCEPTS OF SERVICE DELIVERY AND THE PUBLIC DECISION MAKER

When it comes to alternative management strategies in the public sector, the question is not whether we will see privatization as having a meaningful role, but how this valuable resource can be best applied to a specific problem solution. A survey report by the firm of Touche Ross, published in 1987, "Privatization in America," clearly demonstrates that privatization, both contracted services and privatized facilities, are service delivery options in wide use today across America. In this report, the strongest interest in privatization among governments that had used it in the last five years is the direct result of the demand for services, followed closely by taxpayer resistance to tax increases. When given a choice of responses for the advantages of privatization, the survey respondents placed "cost savings" as the leading advantage followed by "solves labor problems" and then "sharing of risk."

Among governments that had not used privatization, the leading reason for lack of interest was "no apparent cost savings or other benefit" followed by "loss of management control." Unquestionably, privatization must demonstrate a savings or other valuable benefits over equal services from an alternative strategy of service delivery. The issue of loss of management control, as discussed previously, is often more a matter of perception than of reality. The perception can be modified once the process of negotiating a true public-private partnership is undertaken.

The future of local governments in meeting the local needs of their constituencies is summed up well by Ernest N. Morial, former mayor of the city of New Orleans, as follows:

A city is a complex aggregation of individuals and businesses, greater in many ways than the sum of its parts. While privatization is not an answer to all of our financial ills, it is certainly a positive step in utilizing our available resources. The city of the future must be prepared to bring together all potential public and private resources to meet emerging urban demands.

ENVIRONMENTAL INFRASTRUCTURE: A PRIVATIZATION SUCCESS STORY

The success of the privatization alternative, both contracted services and completely privatized facilities, was first seen in managing the solid waste services of our communities. Contracted operation of solid waste collection is now broadly accepted as a sound means of producing that service. The communities' responsibility to provide that service and maintain control has been clearly addressed to the benefit of all.

Today, where capital-intensive refuse-to-energy systems have been proposed as a means of volume reduction for solid wastes, the privatized solution has again been the most popular, and the performance of these facilities has met the expectations of all participants. Within this same environmental infrastructure market, a similar evolution is now occurring in the area of wastewater collection, treatment, and disposal systems. Again, the initial change has occurred in contracted operation of facilities, with the interest and demand for these services growing rapidly for systems of all sizes. More recently, before the Tax Reform Act of 1986, the transition to fully privatized facilities had begun with definite signs of growing interest. Although the Tax Reform Act has slowed this growth, every indication is that the prior successes will challenge the public and private sector at all levels to find ways to continue to move in the direction of fully privatized facilities.

THE PRIVATE SECTOR: FULL SERVICE RESPONSIBILITY

When it comes to fully privatized environmental infrastructure facilities, it is reasonable to ask the question, "What can the private sector do, and why should it make a difference?"

As an overview in considering the response to this question, it is important to keep in mind that the private sector views what it does as its "living." When it engages in providing a service, it does so with very focused attention and a commitment of corporate resources. It also understands that it is always operating in a competitive environment. Finally, it must produce a profit through its efforts as a reasonable return on those committed corporate resources. These points should not be lost as key motivators unique to the private sector.

Structuring of Project Financing

In structuring the financing for a fully privatized facility, the options available are greatly expanded and the impact on the local communities' obligated indebtedness can be greatly minimized. Depending upon the project and prevailing tax law, the financing transaction will differ from traditional public financing, since it will involve some combination of debt and equity capital. In addition, instruments such as industrial development bonds, revenue bonds, or some form of lease transaction may be used.

Unlike the use of traditional general obligation bonds, which are by law considered part of a community's outstanding indebtedness and usually tied to a statutory debt ceiling, these instruments permit the commitment of that limited debt capacity to other uses.

Fundamental to structuring project financing are the guarantees and credit enhancements that are made a part of the deal and that in turn have a favorable impact for the community on the return that bond holders will expect on their money.

Designing for Needs Versus Wants

The private sector has greater flexibility in designing a facility that will accurately meet the current needs of a community while provisions are made for logical future expansions based on usage. During the 1970s and early 1980s when the federal grant programs provided up to 75 percent of project capital needs, the legitimate motivation for communities to "get the money while you can" and therefore build more than you needed, or could afford, was commonplace.

Since no money is "free," with privatization the regulations that come along with grant funding are greatly reduced. In privatization, the harsh realities of actual need, efficiency of operation, and capacity to pay are brought into proper balance. The privatizer also accepts technological innovation, often difficult under government regulation, as a normal business risk because of its potential for saving money. This risk, however, is not passed along to the community.

Construction

The full-service privatizer is a turnkey provider of services. When it comes to privatization requiring capital facilities, the privatizer is by definition a provider of turnkey construction as well, which means on time and within budget as stated in the contract.

The privatizer's selection of subcontractors and plant equipment is based on hands-on knowledge about the subcontractor or equipment. Included in the considerations are such factors as long-term operation of equipment, or demonstrated ability of the subcontractor, not on the lowest bid or on the "or-equal" requirements of public bidding laws.

Subcontractors are more cooperative and open to innovation and change. On typical publicly procured projects, the contractor lacks incentives to cooperate if he knows that future jobs always go to the lowest bidder. But in privatization, he knows that being a good team player may win future contracts. This allows for a fast-track, design-built project that saves money both in construction costs and in the capitalized interest paid during the construction phase.

Guaranteed Performance

In the environmental infrastructure market, it is much too common to see a facility get built and then not have it meet performance specifications. In a traditional public procurement, this is known as the finger-pointing and litigation phase of the project. In privatization, it does not exist. There is only one person responsible: the privatizer.

This is equally true under full privatization and contract operations. Once the performance standards have been mutually agreed and a basis of compensation has been mutually established, the privatizer must perform.

Work-Force Development

The private sector has always recognized the causal relationship between efficient performance and a well-trained work force. Consequently, training and development are high on the list of a privatizer's priorities when it comes to providing full-service responsibilities.

A poorly trained work force will result in substandard facility performance, improper maintenance procedures, excessive use of consumables, and unsafe work habits. All of these are unacceptable in an ongoing business.

Too often, work-force training and development is the first budget item to go in the public sector when "we need to cut back on spending." There is also the concern in the public sector that if you train the work force, you increase their value in the job market, which becomes a double loss, training dollars and personnel. In the private sector, training means opportunity to move up in the company.

Maintenance for Performance

As the investment in work-force development translates into efficient performance, the same can be said for a routine investment in maintenance. The private sector is a true believer in the merits of a comprehensive preventive maintenance program and cannot justify business behavior that suggests that it can be deferred. Like training, this is a common practice in the public sector.

The costliest maintenance is associated with catastrophic failures in a system. By definition, they are unplanned, and therefore they cause the greatest disruption to service and are fixed at a premium cost. Preventive maintenance and scheduled major repairs are the signs of a well-managed environmental infrastructure facility. This behavior is standard for full-service privatizers.

Public Relations

The privatizer views a public image and reputation as critical to the ability to continue being successful in increasing the size of the business. Employees are also members of the community and must feel good about their work and how it is perceived if they are to have a positive attitude at their jobs.

Privatizers seek public interest and concern. They generally believe that the more the public understands about the complexity and critical nature of managing environmental infrastructure, the more supportive they will be when improvements or rate increases are necessary.

INFRASTRUCTURE PRIVATIZATION IS SUCCESSFUL

Privatization of environmental infrastructure, both full-service and contract operation, is growing at a rapid rate. The growth is fueled by the success stories of the early privatization efforts of pioneer communities across the United States. The following is meant only to illustrate the variety of success situations.

Auburn, Alabama

This city needed two entirely new wastewater treatment facilities and significant interceptor sewers. The prospect of grant funding was far enough into the future that it could severely impact the growth of the city and the quality of natural waters in the area.

Under a full-service privatization solution, the new facilities were designed, financed, constructed, and placed in service within eighteen months from the date of bond sale. The project was finished within budget and six months ahead of schedule. The normal period for public facilities using federal grant funds would have been four to five years.

The privatizer assumed operation of the existing facilities during the interim period, trained the staff, and took full responsibility for transition to the new facilities. In addition, the city determined it would save $25 million over the life of the financing compared to a grant-funded project.

Winnsboro, South Carolina

After spending a considerable amount of federal, state, and local money to upgrade its wastewater treatment facilities, the city found itself unable to meet the compliance standards set in their permit. This situation persisted for nearly two years with much political embarrassment and regulatory pressure.

The city decided to turn to contract operations as a means of solving its problems. The results exceeded their expectations. The facility was brought into compliance within thirty days and has continued to comply since that time. The staff was given an intensive training program, which resulted in going from only one certified operator to having the entire staff state certified. The annual contracted price was $90,000 below the city's budget. In addition, the privatizer returned an additional $43,000 to the city after one year of operation from additional savings realized in operating the facilities.

City of Orlando/Orange County, Florida

For many communities the cooperative development of a regional facility is far more cost-effective than the development of smaller facilities serving individual communities. Yet, the difficulties of intermunicipal management of the facilities can become a political nightmare.

In Orlando, Florida, a privatizer is contract operating Water Conserv II, an innovative water reclamation project that is jointly owned by the city of Orlando and Orange County. As an outside service producer responsible to both agencies but "belonging" to neither, the privatizer is able to avoid the potential political problems that might ensue in the operation of the project.

The reclaimed, treated wastewater is distributed to a number of orange growers for irrigation on a regularly scheduled basis by the privatizer and consequently produces revenue. Since the privatizer is motivated to sell as much reclaimed water as possible, it employs one individual whose sole responsibility is to work with customers, identify new customers, and maximize the sale of reclaimed water.

Northwest Suburban Municipal Joint Action Water Agency, Illinois

This seven-member group of communities represents the fastest growing suburban area in Metropolitan Chicago with a combined population of over 250,000 people. These communities had cooperatively implemented a capital program of over $60 million to transport water from the western limits of the city of Chicago an additional twenty-five miles as a source of supply to each of their individually owned and operated distribution systems. Since no one community had the expertise to operate such a large system and in light of some of the potential political conflicts that could result, a privatizer was engaged to contract operate the facilities.

As the end of the five-year operating contract neared, the communities determined that they were now comfortable with operating the system on their own. The privatizer has negotiated a transition plan with the agency, which will ensure no disruption in service. This clearly illustrates that privatization is not an irreversible process and is a management option to serve the public sector.

SELECTION OF A PRIVATIZER

Whether a community has made the decision to proceed with contract operations or full-service privatization, the factors to consider in evaluating potential privatizers are very similar. Although price must be a critical issue in the public procurement process, public officials would be well advised to work with counsel to structure the procurement so that it comforms to state and local law while still allowing for the influence of other key procurement factors. As stated in the local officials' handbook titled *This Way Up* (Armington and Ellis, 1984), "Because of the multiplicity of skills and technical support required for a successful program, 'low bidders' often do not represent the most cost-effective alternative long term."

Expertise

There is specific expertise that a privatizer must be able to demonstrate to local officials to be considered a responsible proposer of services in the area of environmental infrastructure privatization.

Technical/Engineering. Environmental infrastructure involves the application of technology and is based on engineering design. The privatizer who has not invested in this critical expertise as an essential part of the business organization represents a performance risk when conditions in the system change. Being able to analyze the impact of changed conditions and take a proper corrective action is critical in the operation of environmental infrastructure. A privatizer can subcontract to have this expertise included in the service, but unless such subcontracts are ongoing in nature, for the period of the privatization, they will lack the day-to-day relationship needed to assure performance. In full-service privatization, the issue is more pronounced, since this will involve original design, which will lead to major capital expenditures.

Management/Administration. In this area, the privatizer must demonstrate awareness of all management issues and administrative details that go into long-term service delivery contracts. Particularly important is expertise in managing the work force, especially when employees will be transferring to employment by the privatizer.

Directly related to the work-force issues are the privatizer's expertise in working with collective bargaining units. In addition, the privatizer should be able to demonstrate expertise in public relations and communications as an essential element in properly representing the relationship with the local government.

Regulatory. The regulatory issues surrounding environmental infrastructure grow yearly. The interests of the local government and its relations with county, state, and federal regulatory agencies will suffer if the privatizer does not possess the expertise to address all regulatory requirements associated with service delivery. Proper operational reporting, staff certifications, notification of upsets, and accurate performance testing are all important in managing a relationship with a regulatory agency.

Operations and Maintenance. At the heart of the matter is performance, and performance results from a well-established operations and maintenance expertise. If this expertise does not reside within the privatizer's organization, it is questionable whether a serious commitment exists to form a public-private partnership.

A privatizer must first and foremost want to be the producer of the service and must see that function as the reason to be in business. Local officials should evaluate closely any privatizer who subcontracts the actual service delivery function.

Experience

The issue of experience is critical in the selection process but should be considered in such a way as to permit a range of potential privatizers to meet the criteria. Local officials reserve the right to determine qualification based on experience. Experience criteria might include:

- a minimum number of years providing full-service privatization or contract operations
- the operation of facilities of similar complexity or size
- the qualifications of personnel that would be assigned to the facility
- prior success in addressing specific problems similar to those that have existed or may exist at the local facility
- a list of references of all past and current clients

The essential underlying issue is whether the local officials can work with the privatizer to form that essential public-private partnership.

Dedicated Resources

A privatizer's commitment that demonstrates that it is in for the "long haul" can be measured in a number of ways. The following are only a few points that must be carefully assessed.

Human Resources. Service delivery usually comes down to people and performance. Serious privatizers have a human resources management structure that is directed toward serving that work force. An important element of this resource is someone dedicated to dealing with labor relations issues.

Systems. Regulatory reporting and maintenance management at environmental infrastructure facilities are data intensive and need documented systems to keep them accurate and up-to-date. Such systems need not be computer-based, although that is more common, but they must be well thought out and an integral part of management.

Financing. For full-service privatization where capital facilities will need to be financed, it is critical that this resource be clearly identifiable within the management structure of the privatizer's organization. This resource can be supported by outside talent such as investment bankers, but to be a true partner, the privatizer must be able to deal directly with the local officials on matters of project finance.

Career Development. If the measure of commitment is the desire to be in business for the long haul, then a dedicated career development program is a clear indicator of that commitment. The privatizer who is investing in people is also investing in the business and is serious about staying in business. Privatization can offer individuals significant career opportunities without changing employers. Career development fuels that human resource to step up to the challenge.

INFRASTRUCTURE PRIVATIZATION IN SUMMARY

To keep privatization as a rational local consideration within the public sector, it is essential to maintain an innovative management attitude within public administration for alternative service delivery options. The now-antiquated concept that if a community determines that it should provide a service, then it must necessarily produce that service has no place in modern public management.

Environmental infrastructure, which many categorize as a critical and essential service, can be provided through a privatization option without placing the public needs and interests at risk. Essential to providing services in this area is the partnership nature of the contractual relationship. The public partner retains fundamental responsibility for providing the service to the public. In turn, the public should perceive that it is receiving its service from the elected and appointed public officials. The private partner should see interaction with the public as a municipal function where the private partner is acting on behalf of the municipality in performing or producing the service. Only through this concept of partnership can critical environmental infrastructure services be successfully provided. However, it must never be forgotten that the partnership is contractual with a clear division of responsibility and definition of acceptable performance.

Privatization and contract operations were developed as two alternative management strategies. They were not developed to replace the traditional system of public funding, ownership, and operation, but to offer alternatives in those cases where the traditional method was unavailable, economically unfeasible, or inefficient.

It is critical to understand that development by the private sector of privatization and contract operations services was not intended to place the private and public sectors in adversarial roles. The common goal of the public and private sectors is to provide efficient, cost-effective service for the public good. The private sector is not seeking to "replace" the public sector or to subvert the role of government.

It is the genuine belief of responsible privatizers in the area of environmental infrastructure that in some cases, the public-private partnership resulting from privatization and contract operations can achieve the goal of efficient operations more economically, quickly, and dependably than would be possible through other methods and, in those situations, the public is well served by full-service privatization and contract operations.

REFERENCES

Armington, R. Q., and Ellis, W. D. (1984). *This Way Up.* Chicago: Regnery Gateway.

Dobbs, J. C. (1985, Summer). "Rebuilding America: Legal Issues Confronting Privatization," *The Privatization Review* 1, no. 1, 28-38.

Goldman, H. J., and Mokuvos, S. (1984). *The Privatization Book.* New York: Arthur Young.

Savas, E. S. (1982). *Privatizing the Public Sector.* Chatham, NJ: Chatham House Publishing.

6

Privatization of Transportation Services

ROGER F. TEAL

Privatization of various transportation services and facilities has become a serious policy option during the past several years. Not only has there been a noticeable increase in private sector financing and delivery of transportation services and facilities during the 1980s, but the Reagan administration has been a strong supporter of increased levels of transportation privatization. Among the privatization developments of the 1980s have been increased private developer financing of highway (and to a much lesser extent, rail transit) infrastructure; construction of toll highways in four metropolitan areas (Washington, DC, Fort Lauderdale, Tampa-St. Petersburg, and Houston), and plans for toll roads in at least two other areas after two decades in which virtually no urban toll roads were built; and policy initiatives by the federal transit agency to encourage public transit agencies to contract with private transportation operators for at least some of their services. In addition, the federal government orchestrated the sale of Conrail to private investors after spending many billions of dollars to revive the railroad. Some Reagan administration officials have even discussed the privatization of the nation's air traffic control system.

Most of these privatization developments have been motivated at least as much by fiscal circumstances as by ideology. In the 1980s, public funds for both highways and public transportation have been in short supply. Construction and operation costs have increased much more rapidly than have transportation revenue sources (primarily user fees and general taxes), with the result that both highway and transit agencies face fiscal dilemmas in accomplishing their missions. Private sector financing has been viewed as a pragmatic means of enabling highway projects to be constructed, not as necessarily the most desirable method of paying for projects. Similarly, contracting with the private sector to operate public transit services has been promoted as a cost- and subsidy-savings strategy and a means of constraining transit cost increases that otherwise require fare increases, service reductions, or additional tax resources for subsidy.

While almost all aspects of transportation have been affected to some extent by the increased emphasis on privatization, the policy reorientation has been most dramatic for mass transit. A decade ago, the public sector was following implicit policies of ever-increasing subsidy for a monopoly-organized (at the regional/local level) transit industry. Since 1981, however, the Reagan administration has slashed federal assistance to transit by 47 percent in real dollars and, during the past four years, has adopted policies that explicitly encourage competitive procurement of transit services and the abandonment of the public monopoly framework for service delivery. Although these policies have been only partially implemented at the local level and remain intensely controversial, these federal privatization initiatives have had a profound impact on the public transit industry. In contrast, recent highway privatization activities represent simply a greater emphasis on policy actions (developer financing, toll financing) that were already features, albeit less prominent ones, of the urban highway development system. Our analysis, therefore, gives more detailed attention to the policies and actions aimed at privatizing public transportation, as this is the more novel policy development.

PRIVATIZATION OF HIGHWAY DEVELOPMENT

The private sector has always played a role in the financing of the highway system. At the local level, developers have for many years been required to pay for the streets and roads their projects require and occasionally for improvements to existing facilities necessitated by new residential and/or commercial developments. After World War II, until the advent of the 1956 federal highway legislation that established the Interstate system and its financing mechanisms, a vigorous toll-road movement swept the eastern portion of the country. Toll roads were constructed in many states, including most of the northeastern and north central states. Between 1946 and 1965, $7.7 billion was invested in toll roads. While quasi-governmental authorities were responsible for construction and operation of the toll roads, the bonds to finance the roads were sold to private investors. The federal-state partnership to finance the Interstate system, however, gave the states the funds necessary to pay for large-scale highway development, and toll financing quickly lost its attractiveness. The interest on the bonds made toll roads more expensive than roads constructed with gas tax funds. For the next twenty years, public sector financing, based on gasoline tax revenues, was virtually the only way in which nonlocal roads were funded. Even at the local level, most road development except that in residential subdivisions was financed by public revenue sources—gas taxes and local property taxes.

The increasing trend of the past ten years toward private sector financing of highways is largely attributable to the inability of public sector revenue sources to keep pace with highway construction costs. State and federal gas tax revenues have fallen by 11 percent in real dollars since 1970, despite significant increases in the gas tax rate, whereas the construction costs of highways have increased by about 9 percent in real dollars. As a result of this cost-revenue squeeze, most states and localities cannot afford all the highway development they consider desirable, particularly in areas with rapidly growing populations. Consequently, local governments have required larger developer contributions for highways than had been typical in the past. For example, two developers are paying $16 million to Fairfax County, Virginia, for off-site roadway improvements in exchange for zoning changes needed for a large shopping center and office park. While this is a particularly large developer contribution, it is by no means a unique case; contributions of as much as $60 million have been negotiated in other situations.

Developer financing of local highway improvements represents privatization of the highway revenue source, but the highway user perceives no difference in the financing system. Toll roads, however, require a change in how the user pays for road use, namely from the indirect mechanism of the gasoline tax to the direct fee for service system of tolls. Because virtually all adult citizens are road users, this change has been much more controversial politically. Thirty years of "free" freeways have created public expectations about how highways are to be financed; the prospect of toll roads challenges those expectations. The federal government has moved slowly to authorize the use of tolls to finance the state and local share of new federal-aid highways, but has allowed Orange County, California, to create an "experimental" system of planned toll highways, which would be partially financed with federal funds. In those metropolitan areas where toll roads are now being seriously considered or actually constructed—Orange County, Denver, and Houston being the prime examples—the rationale for their development has invariably been that the only realistic alternative to toll roads was no roads, due to lack of funds. Even so, in both Orange County and Denver the political success of the toll road projects is not yet assured.

Increased privatization of highway development is probably a permanent feature of highway financing, but this is not a new financing mechanism and it is not clear how far this trend will progress. Increases in the gasoline tax have been shown to be politically feasible during the past ten years, and significantly large gas tax increases would largely obviate the need for increased levels of developer and toll financing of highways. The question is whether the political will exists to orchestrate gas tax increases of the magnitude that would reverse the trend toward highway privatization.

PUBLIC TRANSPORTATION
PRIVATIZATION DEVELOPMENTS

The primary initiatives for greater privatization of the public transportation industry have come from the leadership of the federal Urban Mass Transportation Administration (UMTA). Throughout the Reagan administration, UMTA's leadership has promoted a larger role for the private sector in service delivery and financing, but serious policy development did not begin until 1984 after the arrival of Ralph Stanley as UMTA administrator. In a series of policy pronouncements, regulations, and grants, Stanley firmly staked out UMTA's privatization policy.

Public transportation represented an almost ideal focus for the Reagan administration's privatization efforts. Public subsidy of the transit industry, initiated on a large scale in the 1960s, unloosed political and economic forces that led to enormous cost escalation in the transit industry. Between 1965 and 1984, the unit costs of the transit industry (cost per vehicle mile of service) rose *140 percent above the rate of inflation*. Since 1975, the first year of federal operating assistance, the hyperinflationary trend has abated, but nonetheless unit costs rose 30 percent above the inflation rate between 1975 and 1984. One analyst estimated that one-third of the increased governmental assistance (in constant dollars) provided to the transit industry between 1975 and 1984 was absorbed by increased labor expenses for existing service, even though labor productivity declined by 7 percent during this period (Pickrell, 1986). Despite an expenditure of $34 billion in operating subsidy by all levels of government during this time period (and $7.6 billion in federal operating subsidies), ridership increased by only 16 percent (and only 6 percent per capita).

Federal operating assistance for transit, therefore, had all the appearances of a classically wasteful and ineffective federal program. Much of the money leaked through into higher real wages for workers whose productivity was actually declining, subsidy requirements were increasing annually (from $1.45 billion in 1975 to $5.75 billion in 1984), and the impact on transit market share was negligible. Moreover, by the early 1980s many transportation analysts outside of both UMTA and the transit industry saw little prospect for changes in this dismal situation without significant changes in the way transit was financed and organized.

UMTA's Privatization Policy

Ralph Stanley was the first UMTA leader to develop and implement a privatization policy that embodied this critical perspective on transit's prospects. This policy initiative had several elements. First, Stanley issued formal policy pronouncements that stated UMTA's intention of strongly encouraging as much private sector operation of transit as possible, primarily through the competitive contracting mechanism, but also through turning over some services to private organizations to operate without subsidy. Second,

UMTA proposed legislation that would have conditioned the level of federal transit subsidies to a region on the amount of service competitively contracted, using UMTA guidelines for the appropriate percentage of contracting. Although Congress rejected this legislative initiative, it revealed Stanley's seriousness of purpose and overall policy intent. Third, using as authority those provisions concerning private operators in the original Urban Mass Transportation Act of 1964, UMTA issued regulations that required all recipients of federal transit funds to develop procedures that would give private operators an opportunity to provide any new or significantly restructured transit services. This essentially required that public transit agencies had to engage in some type of formal evaluation process when determining who should provide such services, up to and including competitive bidding. Fourth, UMTA issued other regulations that enabled federal operating subsidies to be used for purchase of vehicles by private operators who were providing service under contract to public agencies. This capital cost of contracting regulation removed a substantial financial disadvantage for private operators using their own equipment in competing for transit service contracts. Finally, UMTA made a series of grants for both planning studies of privatization and implementation of relatively large-scale competitively contracted services. Stanley also made it clear that regions that took the lead in privatization could expect favored treatment from UMTA on other aspects of their transit program.

The objective of UMTA's privatization policy is no less than a fundamental transformation of the transit service delivery system. Service provision by monopoly-organized public sector transit entities is to be replaced by a system in which private transportation operators, as well as public agencies, operate transit services. In this new system, services do not belong to the established public transit operator; rather, operators are obtained for services through a competitive procurement process. Competitive contracting replaces monopoly service rights as the mechanism for establishing who will operate a service. Significant privatization is anticipated because private operators tend to have significantly lower operating costs than those of public transit agencies, and hence the former will often be selected as service providers in a competitive contracting system.

It is important to emphasize that UMTA's policies are not aimed at returning responsibility for transit to the private sector, where transit ceased being financially viable by the 1960s. UMTA expects that, with few exceptions, services operated by private providers will require public subsidy, and that public agencies will remain responsible for planning, marketing, financing, and monitoring public transit service delivery. Privately operated services will be provided under contract with the public agencies that now receive the funds to subsidize transit operations. In the same manner that many municipal governments contract out a variety of city services while retaining ultimate control, so would the public agencies responsible for transit contract out increasing portions of the transit service delivery system to private operators.

UMTA's private sector policy initiatives thus seek not to turn back transit service provision to the private sector as some uninformed critics have charged, but to create institutional changes that permit private transportation operators to participate in the transit service delivery system in the interests of improved cost effectiveness. Stanley's policy initiatives embody a distinctly different vision of the ideal service delivery mechanism than that in virtually all large U.S. cities. It is precisely this challenge to the institutional structure of transit that has caused the policy to be so controversial. Even though the basic policy of government contracting for service is neither novel nor particularly radical, for the typical medium or large transit agency this federal policy initiative represents a revolutionary departure from previous practice and policies. Thus, it confronts transit managers, policymakers, and organized labor with an unprecedented challenge to a rather comfortable status quo.

UMTA's privatization policy thus poses a clash between two policy imperatives of government: economic efficiency in service production and stable institutional relations. UMTA has firmly taken the side of efficiency and cost effectiveness, but most other actors involved in public transportation have interests that favor economic efficiency to a much smaller degree, if at all. Powerful interests have arisen around the current structure of service provision, and such interests must be either accommodated or their opposition overcome if that structure is to be altered to permit an increased level of service contracting. This reality forms the environment in which this privatization policy is being implemented.

Key Issues of Transit Privatization and Relevant Experiences

The key issues posed by UMTA's attempt to foster increased privatization of the transit industry all relate to this tension between governmental efficiency and changes in institutional structure. These issues can be divided into three broad categories: (1) the potential economic benefits (cost and subsidy savings) of contracting out existing transit agency services, (2) the institutional feasibility of large-scale privatization activities, and (3) the impacts on both transit agencies and private transportation operators of a service delivery system that is largely based on contracting. Each of these issues, and the empirical evidence bearing on them, is considered below.

Potential Economic Impacts of Privatization. Because the most compelling rationale for promoting service contracting is the potential cost and subsidy savings of such a policy, much attention has focused on the likely magnitude of such savings. Of the relatively few studies that have been conducted, most have estimated cost savings in the range of 10 to 50 percent (Teal et al., 1984; Southern California Association of Governments, 1982; Herzenberg, 1983; McKnight and Paaswell, 1984; Teal, 1986; Teal et al., 1988). A variety of methodologies have been employed to estimate these cost differences between public agencies and private contractors, ranging from simple comparisons of unit costs to the use of relatively sophisticated cost models. The most extensive of these studies, which provided cost impact analyses for twenty-two transit systems, estimated actual transit agency service costs using an avoidable cost model, but was forced to rely on estimates of private operator costs for the same services. This study determined that transit systems of 150 or more vehicles would save 5 to 50 percent of service costs for fixed-route bus services that they contract (Teal et al., 1988), with mean savings of 27 percent. With 20 percent of the agency's total service contracted, the systemwide cost savings averaged about 5.5 percent, and the subsidy savings averaged about 9 percent.

The same authors conclude, however, that the magnitude of cost savings is highly dependent on the service and fiscal characteristics of the public agency and that the cost differential between public and private operators of small transit systems is relatively small (Teal et al., 1988). Moreover, the transit industry has challenged the validity of all estimates of cost savings currently cited, contending that private operator cost levels will rise rapidly to those of existing public agencies.

Because almost all transit contracting to date has involved services that were never operated by public agencies, the cost analyses have necessarily been of a "what if" nature. Thus, while the analyses have rather consistently indicated that significant cost savings will occur if services are contracted out, the paucity of empirical data invariably weakens them. The experience of Yolo County, California, where an entire transit system was contracted first to the Sacramento regional transit district and then to a private operator, with a documented 38 percent cost savings by the latter, is a relatively unique example of a shift of existing services from public sector operation (Teal, 1986).

The cost savings issue is crucial to the fate of the private sector policy initiatives, as many policymakers will condition their support on what "the numbers" indicate are the payoffs from a policy of private sector contracting.

Institutional Feasibility of Large-Scale Privatization. Private sector contracting for transit service is already a phenomenon of significant import, but primarily for small-scale transit service. A recent survey of 864 transit operations found that 35 percent of all systems contract for some or all of their service (Teal et al., 1988). Although the majority of service contracting is for demand-responsive transit (DRT), a substantial amount also occurs for fixed-route transit. More than 150 public agencies (22 percent of all fixed-route systems nationwide) contract for fixed-route transit.

The bulk of contracted service delivery occurs in small transit systems, over 70 percent in systems of fifty or fewer vehicles. When large transit agencies engage in service contracting, it is almost invariably for a limited service—typically a specialized DRT service for the elderly and handicapped—which represents a small fraction of their total service. This pattern of contracting explains why expenditures on contracted services represent only 5 percent of national transit operating expenditures and contracted service constitutes only 9 percent of total service miles.

Consequently, only a handful of public transportation agencies contract for a substantial amount of service. Moreover, there is even less *competitive* service contracting for large-scale services. Several major institutional obstacles confront UMTA's attempts to alter this situation.

First, the policy initiatives for increased contracting have emanated from the federal level, but the policy subsystem for public transportation is distinctly nonhierarchical. Service and organizational decisions about transit are made at the local level, and the bulk of transit operating subsidies are nonfederal in origin. (Federal subsidies represent less than 15 percent of the total subsidies.) UMTA lacks the legal authority and the policy legitimacy to dictate to local transit authorities how they organize their service delivery system. In fact, its efforts to use administrative regulations to force greater consideration of contracting have provoked restrictive congressional language in budget appropriations. Without question, UMTA's policy initiatives have substantially altered the decision-making environment for service delivery organization, but this does not ensure that transit agencies will actually significantly increase their use of service contracting. The latter outcome is primarily a function of local conditions.

Labor issues are another major component of the institutional feasibility of large-scale transit contracting. Labor unions are at present adamantly opposed to dismantling the monopoly structure for transit service provision, and they are unlikely to change this posture. While increased levels of service contracting can be phased in in such a way that no existing transit workers lose their jobs, transit unions are major losers if service contracting expands significantly. There will be fewer unionized transit workers (and hence less union dues), a much reduced union influence with management and the transit policy board, and in all likelihood strong pressures to make concessions on wages and work rules to bring public agency costs more in line with those of private contractors. Moreover, the prospects for organizing the employees of the private contractor are not particularly bright, as a policy of competitive procurement of services will favor private companies with low to moderate wages. As union organization has typically been associated with high wage levels, unions may be forced to adjust their monetary objectives sharply if they wish to have any opportunity to organize workers at private companies.

The labor protections embodied in Section 13(c) of the Urban Mass Transportation Act are frequently cited as a major impediment to an increased level of private sector contracting. Actually, nothing in the language of Section 13(c) per se constrains the ability of transit agencies to engage in service contracting, provided that *existing* transit employees are not directly displaced as a result. Thus, a phased policy of increased contracting that works within the agency's attrition rate for impacted employees will not run afoul of 13(c) itself. Section 13(c), however, has created a labor-management bargaining situation in which federal law mandates collective bargaining as the means for altering the terms of labor contracts, many of which in the transit industry contain severe or absolute restrictions against service contracting. Even when such contracts are silent on the issues of subcontracting, management's right to engage in subcontracting must usually be either bargained for with labor or awarded through arbitration, both of which are problematic procedures. Until management has the clear right to engage in service contracting, the affected transit agencies will have little or no opportunity to increase the level of service contracting.

The casual observer of public transit might suppose that transit management would welcome a policy promoting increased transit contracting, as this would increase management flexibility and clout in its relations with its unionized workers. In fact, many managers are reluctant to embrace service contracting. For twenty or more years, public monopoly status has protected transit management from the rigors of the competitive marketplace. Many managers, particularly those with long tenure in the transit industry, have developed a personal and ideological stake in the current system of service delivery. They believe public monopoly to be both necessary and desirable, and find privatization to be a major threat to established managerial style. Moreover, accommodations have been made with labor in the name of stable labor relations. The absence of competitive market forces has enabled transit managers to accept wage levels and work rules that would not be sustainable in the competitive private sector. Furthermore, public monopoly status affords management significant political clout, for the agency is the sole provider of an important public service and employs hundreds or even thousands of unionized workers, who themselves are important local political interests. Transit policy boards usually defer to the advice of management when making important decisions, as the latter is perceived as most knowledgeable in view of its monopoly on transit operating expertise. The prospect of significantly increased levels of service contracting thus presents transit management with a severe personal, political, and organizational dilemma, given the far-reaching managerial changes implied by an acceptance of this prospect.

The policy-level organization of public transit at the local level also poses a major challenge to the institutional feasibility of increased service contracting. The prime benefit of contracting is cost—and subsidy—reduction, but these reductions have *political* advantage only if they can be translated into taxpayer benefits, such as lower taxes or improved service. When the governmental structure that provides transit exists only to perform that function (as with special districts) or when the agency's savings cannot be applied to other local services or to a reduction in overall local tax burden—as when local subsidy sources are dedicated *exclusively* to transit—then policymakers have no compelling motivation to reduce service costs to the lowest possible level commensurate with adequate service. In fact, if such cost reductions are not necessitated simply to keep the service in existence, they represent a political liability because of the adverse reaction by organized labor interests.

When fiscal incentive structures do make high transit costs a political disadvantage, the effect on the service delivery system can be significant. The public transit situation in San Diego County provides one of the most compelling examples of this phenomenon, illustrating the widespread appeal of service contracting when a regional transit authority does not have a legally mandated monopoly on service delivery. Historically, no transit authority in San Diego has had region-wide jurisdiction. San Diego Transit is a city-owned public corporation with a monopoly on service provision only in the city of San Diego. Suburban cities and the county of San Diego can obtain local transit service in any way they desire. The suburban cities contract with San Diego Transit for some trunkline service *through* their communities, but all local service (both fixed-route and DRT) is obtained from private sector operators, as is commuter and all-day bus service *into* San Diego from the southern suburbs. The county of San Diego contracts with private operators for all the local and commuter service under its jurisdiction (in unincorporated areas and for some long-distance commuter service), at a unit cost about one-third less than that of San Diego Transit. Although a regional authority for transit has recently been created, it has opted not to operate services and has no intention of "publicizing" local transit in suburban areas. Moreover, the regional authority is giving serious consideration to contracting out some of San Diego Transit's commuter bus services. The regional transit authority views its responsibility as ensuring that an adequate level of transit is provided in a cost-effective fashion, and transit service contracting is one important tool for achieving that objective.

Few large regional transit authorities, however, operate under fiscal incentive systems like those in San Diego. Most have dedicated sources of local or state subsidy, and enjoy a monopoly on service provision in their service district. Not surprisingly, the typical large agency has rather high costs and does little service contracting. The fiscal arrangements for transit funding thus constitute an important environmental influence on local perceptions of the desirability of transit service contracting.

Impacts of Large-Scale Privatization on Service Delivery. The final set of issues concerns the impact of large-scale service contracting on the transit service delivery system and the participants in that system. Of course, the spector of undesirable impacts—at least from a self-interested point of view—motivates certain interests to oppose contracting, but there are a number of other relevant impacts as well. Will private contractors perform to the level of quality that the public agency has established as a standard for transit service in the region? What incentives and/or disincentives are needed to insure an acceptable level of quality? Will unions organize the employees of private transportation operators who contract with public agencies, and if so, what will be the impacts on costs? Relatedly, can private operator cost levels be maintained over time (in real terms), or will they sharply increase as the transit industry contends? Will increased service contracting opportunities stimulate the creation of a strong private operator supply system, thereby ensuring that competitive forces will be present? What changes in transit agency compensation levels and labor practices are likely if private operators establish lower benchmark cost levels by using different wage rates and work rules from those prevailing in the public transit industry? And what will be the impact on transit agency cost levels if a significant amount of service contracting occurs? Because of the limited experience with large-scale service contracting, definitive answers to these questions are not available. Nonetheless, the widespread experiences with small-scale transit contracting, and the few experiences with larger-scale contracting which have occurred, offer some insights into these issues.

Transit industry critics of privatization almost invariably contend that service quality will suffer if services are contracted to private operators. In fact, contracted service delivery *is* prone to quality control problems if service specifications are ambiguous and monitoring is lax. Some service sponsors have had problems with service quality under such circumstances. The experience of Riverside (California) Transit Authority illustrates the typical response to such problems. Riverside contracts for a sizable amount of DRT and fixed-route service (involving more than twenty-five vehicles at one point in time). When problems with service quality began, Riverside's management did two things. First, it informed contractors that inadequate service quality would result in contract termination and in one case actually terminated a contractor. Second, it substantially altered its contracts to give greater incentives for service quality and to share more financial risks with its contractors. It also instituted more stringent reporting requirements. These actions reduced the magnitude of the quality problem to acceptable levels. Riverside's management believes, and most agencies that have contracted for service for some time concur, that the quality of service obtained depends largely on the quality of the contractual arrangement itself. When the contract is unambiguous and contractor performance is adequately monitored, sponsors usually believe that they receive what they pay for.

A second major contention of privatization critics is that contractor cost levels will quickly rise to public transit agency levels if large-scale contracting occurs. It is believed that a major cause of such cost increases will be unionization of private operator employees (who are usually not unionized), with a concomitant increase in compensation rates. The experience of relatively large-scale DRT services is not consistent with these hypotheses. In large-scale programs in Orange County (California) and San Bernardino County (California), unionization has not occurred and service costs have actually increased less rapidly than the rate of inflation (Teal, 1985). DRT drivers tend to receive low wages ($4 and $6 per hour), however, and may not be attractive targets for unionization.

In Snohomish County, Washington, the drivers of a contractor for a relatively large fixed-route service were successfully organized by a transit union and did manage to negotiate somewhat higher wage rates. Because the contract was competitively awarded and is subject to competitive rebidding after three years, management has apparently persuaded the union that any higher compensation levels will result in the ultimate loss of the contract, and with it the employees' jobs. The prospect of competitive contract renewals thus places a constraint on union wage demands and operator cost levels, which has been absent in the monopoly-organized public transit industry. This probably explains why examples of rapid cost escalation by contractors do not seem to exist.

Large-scale service contracting is premised on an adequate supply of operators to establish workable competition (or at least contestability) for contracts. The element of competition, after all, is what prevents the adverse economic consequences of a monopoly-organized service delivery system. In most regions, adequate competition exists for DRT contracts, due to the availability of local taxi operators as well as, in some locales, specialized DRT contractors. However, it is not uncommon for only three to five companies to bid on relatively large-scale fixed-route contracts, with some bids having very high prices. Moreover, there are only three or four companies that are capable of bidding on fixed-route contracts throughout the country. In Great Britain, where competitive contracting is now required for all subsidized transit services outside London and for an increasing portion of bus service in the London region, typically only a few private operators bid on services. Given that the number of competitors appears to be merely adequate, not abundant, at a relatively low level of fixed-route contracting, it is not clear what impact a large increase in service contracting would have on competition. If the availability of higher levels of contract revenues did not stimulate additional entry into the contracting market, competition for any one contract could become minimal as major contractors divided up the market in oligopolistic fashion.

Finally, the impact of relatively high levels of contracting on transit agency labor practices and cost levels is an important unknown. The indirect impacts of contracting on agency cost levels could easily exceed the direct cost savings if transit management can use the threat of increased privatization to induce its union(s) to negotiate lower wage rates (at least for new employees) and less restrictive work rules. That this *might* occur is indicated by the experience of Tidewater Transit in Norfolk, Virginia, where management implemented a policy of converting low-ridership bus service to privately contracted DRT or fixed-route van service. An econometric analysis by Talley and Anderson (1986) found that increases in the amount of service Tidewater contracted out were associated with reductions in the cost of services operated in-house by the transit agency. This occurred because Tidewater was able to win important concessions on wage rates and work rules due to the drivers union's concern about the loss of jobs from large-scale service contracting.

A recent study by the Urban Institute (Peterson et al., 1986) gives some insight into the potential scope of these indirect impacts. The study found that among private sector bus drivers in eight large cities, annualized compensation levels were an average of 21 percent (for unionized drivers) to 45 percent (for nonunion drivers) less than for the transit agency drivers in the same cities.

Surprisingly, compensation differentials were even greater for mechanics. These results, moreover, do not consider the impact of productivity, which is probably lower in the public sector due to traditional restrictive work rules. Although it is implausible that public sector wages and work rules will be altered to conform precisely to those in the private sector, this study does indicate that the indirect cost impacts induced by contracting may be significant indeed.

CONCLUSIONS

Increased privatization of both the highway and public transit system has occurred during the 1980s. In both cases, fiscal concerns have been a major stimulus for the development, although ideology has also played a major role in the Reagan administration's embrace of transit privatization. It is too early to assess the durability of these privatization developments, but a return to the almost total public sector reliance of the mid-1970s is unlikely. The transit privatization initiative has been the more politically controversial of the developments to date, but toll financing of highways could also arouse substantial opposition if it became a more widely advocated policy option.

The controversy surrounding transit privatization illustrates the extreme difficulty of changing government service-delivery structures once an activity has been thoroughly institutionalized in the public sector. The debate over whether the private sector should play a significantly larger role in transit service delivery is perhaps the most far-reaching policy debate affecting transit since its move into the public sector in the 1960s. While the outcome of that debate is very much in question, the issues it raises go to the heart of the question of how local services are best delivered. The outcome will tell us a great deal about the relative strength of those interests associated with established program claimants and those interests seeking to reduce government budgets through structural changes in program delivery systems.

REFERENCES

Herzenberg, A. (1983). *Who Should Run Boston's Buses?* Unpublished M.S. thesis, Massachusetts Institute of Technology.

McKnight, C. E., and R. E. Paaswell (1984). *Cost Analysis: Selected Routes.* Final Report, Transit Study Corp. Chicago, Ill: Urbana Transportation Center.

Peterson, G. E., W. G. Davis, Jr., and C. Walker (1986). *Total Compensation of Mass Transit Employees in Large Metropolitan Areas.* Final report prepared for the Urban Mass Transportation Administration (Project UI-3531). Washington, DC: Urban Institute.

Pickrell, D. H. (1986). "Federal Operating Assistance for Urban Mass Transit: Assessing a Decade of Experience." *Transportation Research Record,* 1078: 1-10.

Southern California Association of Governments (1982). *Commuter and Express Bus*

Service in the SCAG Region: A Policy Analysis of Public and Private Operations. Los Angeles, CA: Southern California Association of Governments, Transit Section.

Talley, W. K., and E. E. Anderson (1986). "An Urban Transit Firm Providing Transit, Paratransit, and Contracted-out Service," *Journal of Transport Economics and Policy,* 20, no. 3, 353-368.

Teal, R. F. (1985). "Private Enterprise in Public Transportation: The Case of the Taxi Industry," *Transportation Quarterly* 39, no. 2 (April).

Teal, R. F. (1986). "Transit Service Contracting: Experiences and Issues," *Transportation Research Record,* 1036: 28-36.

Teal, R. F., G. M. Giuliano, M. E. Brenner, S. B. Rooney, and J. K. Jacobs (1984). *Private Sector Options for Commuter Transportation,* Final Report for the Urban Mass Transportation Administration. Washington, DC: Government Printing Office.

Teal, R. F., G. M. Giuliano, J. Golob, and E. W. Morlok (1988). *Cost Impacts of Public Transit Service Contracting,* Final Report to the Urban Mass Transportation Administration. Washington, DC: U.S. Government Printing Office.

7

Privatization of Fire Protection and Beyond by Rural/Metro

JOHN A. TURNER

Rural/Metro Corporation, headquartered in Scottsdale, Arizona, did not hold a lot of promise when its founder, Lou Witzeman, wrestled with establishing it as a fire service over forty years ago in a rural area that is now part of metropolitan Phoenix. Today fire protection is one of two primary emergency services that the company delivers. Last year the revenue mix showed the company's ambulance operations ahead of fire for the first time with 47 percent of the company's gross revenue versus 44 percent for fire operations. (The balance comes from its home health care and security operations.) These figures, however, do not reflect any less interest in fire operations, only that there is more opportunity and less controversy in seeking ambulance contracts. Revenue has increased at the rate of 33 percent per year since 1981.

In February 1948 founder Lou Witzeman's thoughts on the future of Rural/Metro did not extend beyond the next ninety days. At that time he was primarily trying to fill a potential crisis in his life and his home: lack of fire protection. Witzeman had no master plan in forming the company; however, he needed fire protection and was determined to get it.

Pursuing a desperate plan and armed with promises from his neighbors to pay him $10 a month for fire protection, Witzeman invested his last $900 in a fire truck only to find that the promises did not convert to cash and he was stuck with a fire truck. Witzeman learned something that every twenty-one-year-old in this world should know. One cannot count on neighbors. When you go to collect, no one pays.

Witzeman had two choices: either go into business or go bankrupt. Fortunately he decided to tough it out, and with one fire truck, four men, and a modest budget he began a subscription fire service. Applying brains, hard work, and a little luck, he grossed $30,000 the first year. Last year Rural/Metro had gross revenues exceeding $41 million from a range of emergency services provided to fifty communities in five states.

SCOTTSDALE, ARIZONA: THE FIRST PRIVATE CONTRACT

There has always been a chemistry between the leadership of Scottsdale and Rural/Metro. It was the cornerstone for innovative thinking, planning, and implementation of ideas—the key to a unique partnership. It was there from the beginning when, in 1951, the newly incorporated city, with only 2,000 residents, became the first to buck tradition by contracting with a nontraditional private fire protection company. Witzeman cites that contract as the key to the success of the company. Scottsdale today is a nationally recognized progressive resort city that has successfully blended the charm of the Old West with innovative community planning.

Scottsdale encouraged innovative thinking, according to Witzeman. He felt that in order to succeed, he had to provide better service than the traditional public fire departments. His people had to be more than just good firefighters; they had to be good businessmen as well. Indeed, breaking with tradition by applying innovative concepts and operations to the delivery of fire protection in combination with a hard-sell prevention ethic became Rural/Metro's trademark. Underlying the company's success is its ability to deliver cost-effective fire protection in combination with increased productivity.

Witzeman's early philosophy of matching the personnel to the fire load, avoiding overkill, remains with the company today as its key operational concept among its twenty-five fire departments. This concept has been met with both awe and disdain among the traditionalists as well as other segments of the population who cannot part with the notion that fire departments must necessarily be a function of government.

Simply put, the system employs full-time firefighters backed by paid on-call reserves. Not keeping people at work for the worst case scenario—as traditional fire protection delivery often does—results in a more productive, cost-effective system, tailored to meet the requirements of its contracting communities. The reserves get paid only when called out to fight a fire or to attend training sessions. The resulting savings, combined with a longer work week than union fire departments, make for greater efficiencies and productivity.

The Master Contract

Today, Scottsdale contracts with Rural/Metro under a ten-year master contract with the company providing equipment and all full-time personnel for fire prevention, suppression, and building and fire code inspections, as well as arson investigations and public education programs. The city specifies the staffing for each twenty-four-hour shift, maintenance workers, communications center dispatching, and administrative staff.

The city also specifies what equipment the contractor will own and what equipment the city will own as well as the numbers of fire stations needed and their locations. Currently Rural/Metro owns approximately 50 percent of the fire protection equipment. Rural/Metro provides expert counsel in the development of these specifications and in the overall decision-making process relevant to all aspects of fire protection.

The Rural/Metro fire suppression staff is augmented by an auxiliary program using city employees, who are trained in basic fire techniques, including ladder and hose. During periods of training and fire suppression activity, the auxiliaries, known as fire support specialists, are under the general supervision of the Rural/Metro fire operations staff.

To assist the city staff in supervising the activities and effectiveness of the fire service, Rural/Metro provides the city with monthly and annual reports. The company also maintains substantial general liability insurance to protect the city.

The city sets minimum response times and monitors the contract with Rural/Metro, receiving an advance monthly set retainer for service. This retainer is determined annually during the city's budgeting process.

Why Does It Work?

The program works because both parties significantly benefit from the contractual relationship on a relatively equal basis. Therefore, there is no reason for either party to risk termination of the relationship. This program can only be effective if a relationship of trust exists. This is not to say that supervision of the contractor is not desired. The contractor wants and deserves supervision. Only by knowing the desires of the city can the contractor satisfy those desires.

No Bidding Process

The contract has been consistently renewed without going through the competitive bidding process, simply because the city is pleased with Rural/Metro's service and the cost savings it provides. This arrangement has met political opposition from the public fire departments in surrounding communities and elsewhere. While Scottsdale has become a national model for its nontraditional approach to fire protection, it also has become the target of the national firefighters union because of its break with tradition. Figures provided by the National Fire Protection Association show that Scottsdale's average per capita cost is about half of what it is for small cities in general.

Practicing the Prevention Ethic

The company's ability to demonstrate its fire prevention ethic through farsighted innovative fire codes while setting national standards and models in the process is a dramatic example of what the private and a public sector can do when each can work toward the public good with well-researched, if not always popular, thinking and planning. By working very closely with the Scottsdale City Council over the years Rural/Metro was able to impact the city's development by engineering strict fire codes and the nation's most comprehensive commercial and residential sprinkler ordinances.

Progressive leadership, tough building and fire codes, and the unique partnership between Scottsdale and its private fire department have seen the city evolve into a well-planned, nationally recognized, progressive resort community of over 110,000 residents. Moreover, it has become one of the most structurally fire-safe cities in the country. For example, Scottsdale passed a fire code in 1974 requiring sprinklers in commercial buildings. That code remains strictly enforced.

While pleased with this success, Bob Edwards, Scottsdale fire chief and a vice president for Fire-Line of Business wanted to take the fire code a giant step farther, right into the home. In mid-1985, Edwards persuaded the Scottsdale City Council to adopt what he called the most comprehensive fire code in the world. The city's ordinance requires an automatic sprinkler system in every room of every commerical, industrial, and residential building in the city. The ordinance applies to all new multifamily residential and commercial buildings, as well as all single-family homes and subdivisions. Chief Edwards called it the twenty-four-hour firefighter.

It did not come easily. Edwards had first considered a similar ordinance six years earlier, but due to considerable resistance, had to put it on the back burner. But in 1982 he arranged a national test of two types of new quick-response sprinkler heads after convincing a Scottsdale builder to retro-fit two homes with them. Rural/Metro assumed full liability for the houses.

Over 250 interested parties from throughout the country and overseas attended what became a dramatic breakthrough test of life-saving, quick-response sprinklers for use in the home. It was the first test of its kind with people sitting in a room without protective gear while a fire challenged a sprinkler system. It proved you could be in a room with a fire until it was extinguished by the sprinklers and not suffer carbon monoxide poisoning, disorientation, or be overcome by heat.

Edwards and Rural/Metro Corporation President Ron Butler persuaded the city council members and building officials to witness the drama, and the test became the nucleus of the new sprinkler ordinance. Edwards drafted the ordinance that placed life safety ahead of building safety in a working reality and began a successful public education campaign to overcome skepticism and natural resistance to change. That ordinance remains a national model for other communities, some of which have adopted it in whole or in part.

Creating the Niche of Private Fire Service

Ironically, it is the public sector fire service that provided an expanding niche for the private sector fire service. Lou Witzeman did not consider the reasons how when he founded Rural/Metro four decades ago. They were not important then or as prevalent as they were to become. But he has thought about it since. In an article for a handbook for local officials considering privatization, *This Way Up* (Armington and Ellis, 1984), Witzeman summarizes his philosophy on the public fire service. It is a philosophy at the foundation of the Rural/Metro success story to the degree that the company broke with tradition.

THE HIGH COST OF WAITING FOR SOMETHING TO HAPPEN

Witzeman asserts that the romantic if very expensive era gave way to a period of professionals. Other new factors in the equation were taxpayer protest and private competition. A major deterrent to competitive private providers has been the difficulty of measuring the effectiveness of a unit that spends most of its time waiting for the largest thinkable disaster, which almost never happens.

To evaluate a fire services action, one must estimate what would have happened had the unit not been there. Fire losses per capita or per dollar at risk are useful but are faulty because no two communities are alike. The measurement problem plus willing taxpayers allowed fire service budgets to go virtually uncontested.

Further contributing to the enviable status of little control over budgets were these factors: firemen were the government's "good guys" (they irritated no one, in contrast to policemen or street construction workers); firemen were heroic and acquired a mystique. The mystique developed around the majestic red truck and the imposing uniforms. Before Proposition 13, fire services added paramedicine services. The television show *Emergency* popularized paramedicine during that time.

Witzeman sold the company to its employees in 1978 through an Employee Stock Ownership Plan (ESOP), which provided a smooth transition of ownership while providing Witzeman a retirement income. Witzeman currently serves as chairman emeritus of the company board of directors, making him available for consultation as the company continues it rapid growth and expansion. Under the ESOP employees have seen the value of their stock increase from $10.31 per share to $158 per share today. All employees are automatically enrolled and pay nothing into the plan.

As a successful pioneer in privatization of such a traditionally public service Rural/Metro has attracted a lot of attention and scrutiny over the years from various levels of government, universities, investigative journalists, study groups, and various others. Each year the company receives hundreds of calls from across the country from people or groups that are just curious about how

Rural/Metro works or from various government entities that want to understand Rural/Metro for privatization contract consideration.

THE HARVARD STUDY

In 1981 the Harvard University Graduate School of Business Administration class did a case study of Rural/Metro. Student analysis concluded that while the company's flexible response concept, its innovative management, and enhanced productivity were paramount to the success the company has enjoyed, product proliferation and expansion beyond its current market areas were not feasible. This conclusion was supported by analysis that determined the company was undercapitalized and short on business management staffing necessary to reach beyond its current borders of business. The history of the corporation since that study does not support the analysis. Indeed, much expansion has occurred. Capital and credit have been forthcoming. Growth in terms of new business, additional employees, new markets, new products and services, and gross revenues has been phenomenally successful.

RURAL/METRO TODAY

Growing from one fire truck and four men in 1948, Rural/Metro is celebrating four decades of excellence with a fleet of over 400 vehicles and over 1,800 employees collectively known as "The Emergency People." Its contracts range from $160,000 to over $3 million annually for periods ranging in length from one to ten years. The company has over 95,000 fire subscription and 30,000 ambulance subscription customers comprising individual homeowners and businesses. Certified as one of the top 100 corporations in Arizona, Rural/Metro today serves 5 million people throughout 22,000 square miles of America.

In combination with the company's full-time/part-time paid reserve system is an ambitious fleet service program that provides not only major maintenance and refurbishing of its vehicles, but also fire truck and equipment construction when needed. The company also contracts with ten fire districts throughout Arizona. (A fire district is a special-purpose governmental body with limited powers that can be created by residents in a given area to address their fire protection needs.)

As a marketing strategy the company will expand its ambulance care to areas adjacent to existing operations throughout its various geographic regions. This not only meets expansion goals but also permits the sharing of administrative and management costs. Of course, the company still relies on its time-tested door-to-door sales for fire and ambulance subscriptions supported by specialized advertising and direct mail. The company does not seek municipal fire protection contracts, preferring instead to respond to serious queries from various government entities. Such, however, is not the case in ambulance operations. Rural/Metro does seek potential ambulance contracts by making contact with key political entities in targeted states confined mostly to the

the city for its representative to monitor events and inform and educate the public on privatization and Rural/Metro. In mid-November the company contracted with an advertising agency and commissioned a public opinion survey to ascertain views on privatization.

In tandem with these actions, the company's representative began interviewing members of the city council from whom Rural/Metro could reasonably expect to see a Request for Proposal (RFP) on a one-on-one basis to determine the extent of their support for privatizing the fire department. Reaction from the council was mixed but encouraging. While some members were noncommittal, none were categorically against the concept.

The scientific sampling of the population revealed, as expected, that the public knew very little about privatization and nothing about Rural/Metro beyond the fabrications provided by the union. The company was determined to change that. A press conference was called on December 10 that attracted media within a one hundred-mile radius of the city. The privatization issue had become a media event and the biggest political issue in recent memory for this small community. Charges and countercharges between the union and the city were making daily headlines while the union continued its picketing activities. This, together with the mobile anti-privatization sign, continued to be the focal point around which media activity galvanized. Frequent city edicts that the union "cease and desist" seemed to play into the hands of the union and whet the appetite of the media.

The Rural/Metro news conference was held across the street from city hall on the same day as a scheduled evening meeting of the city council. In an effort to upstage Rural/Metro, the union beefed up its picket line in front of city hall with wives and children of city firefighters. That evening the union presented the council with citizens' petitions calling for a referendum on the privatization issue.

A Rural/Metro spokesman told a packed press conference that privatization was essentially an economic issue and that the company's concept of operations provided a more cost-effective and productive alternative to traditional fire protection delivery. Although some media bias in favor of the city fire department was evident, on, balance, the reporting was fair.

Through one-on-one media interviews and speaking engagements before local civic groups—such as the Lions and Kiwanis clubs—Rural/Metro's spokesman continued to hammer away at the cost-effective, increased productivity benefits of a private fire department of the city. These groups were very receptive to the concept of privatization and the prospect of saving money, which Rural/Metro virtually guaranteed under its concept of operations.

The union, on the other hand, was taking the approach that only a public fire department that did not have to deal with profit considerations could really "care." "We Care" became the logo in their advertising and on T-shirts that union firefighters and their families and supporters wore at every opportunity. The real, emotional issue for the union membership, however, was fear, fear of losing their jobs if the city converted to a private fire department. This fear was not entirely unfounded, since Rural/Metro's concept of operations requires fewer full-time firefighters than municipal union fire departments, through the use of its paid on-call reserves to augment the full-timers as needed. On this subject the company decided to launch an advertising blitz to run over a thirty-day period beginning December 15. At the conclusion of this multimedia campaign a second public opinion survey would be taken to measure the effectiveness of the advertising and its impact on changing public opinion. Since the first survey had indicated that nearly a third of the population were retirees, the advertising would present an emotional message specific to their needs and concerns for emergency protection. The initial survey had also suggested a need for a relatively high level of education, which permitted the advertising to present a fairly complex message to an audience who could grasp its meaning and impact.

Rural/Metro representatives contracted with an advertising agency in a nearby community to plan the campaign. Models were cast and photographed to present an emotional appeal involving an emergency that everyone could identify with, a residential fire. The advertising (Figs 7.1 and 7.2) also emphasized the cost savings and increased productivity that Rural/Metro could deliver without compromising quality of service or response times.

Three newspaper, two radio, and one television advertisement were developed. On December 15 ads began running in three key area newspapers and on three radio stations. The thirty-second television commercial ran over 300 times on cable television.

Objectives of the Advertising Campaign

Major goals of the campaign were to:

- Educate the public on the issue of privatization.
- Encourage community support for privatization and Rural/Metro.
- Create favorable public attitudes, so that the city council would feel justified in approving a contract with Rural/Metro.
- Counter erroneous information distributed by the union.

Upon completion of the advertising/public relations campaign, the second survey was conducted to assess any changes in the public's awareness and opinions on the issue of privatization versus municipal union fire protection.

Results

Results of the campaign were encouraging:

- The awareness level of the voting public increased dramatically between the time of the first and the second survey.

Rural/Metro...saving money, saving lives

You probably don't give your local fire department a second thought—until you need them. Then a quick response could mean saving thousands of dollars in property—or saving a life. Rural/Metro is a private company that will make your current fire protection more efficient *and* more cost-effective. We hire local qualified firefighters and maintain the excellent level of service you've come to expect—but at less cost. In fact, we can cut the cost of what you're now paying for fire protection by as much as 25% each year...that's about $300,000. Support the change to Rural/Metro in Fort Walton Beach...quality fire protection you can live with.

Figure 7.1

Can you tell the difference between a city firefighter and a private Rural/Metro firefighter?

CITY-OWNED	RURAL/METRO
Quality of Service	
Costly... full-time manpower.	Delivers more manpower to the fire scene. Hires local qualified firefighters. Nationally recognized for fire prevention. Innovative leadership since 1948.
Relations w/ Government	
Union negotiates with city.	Contracts by competitive process. No union. Teamwork—community partnership.
Employee Incentives	
Union represented.	Employee ownership stimulates and promotes responsive. cost effective services.

But the big difference is...
HOW MUCH IT COSTS YOU!

Cost to Taxpayers

Escalating costs have increased 40% over the past 4 years.	Fair... Rural/Metro will reduce costs. Estimated savings of $300,000 per year.

The Emergency People

Figure 7.2

- People were aware of Rural/Metro's advertising campaign and the push for privatization.

- The increase in those favoring privatization was not significant; however, those opposed to the change dropped dramatically to less than 50 percent of those opposed in the first survey.

- Most people believed a private firm would be more cost-effective. (This seemed to be the most significant change.)

- Other results showed a considerable drop in public support of unionization in the fire department and an overall increased receptiveness toward privatization.

Rural/Metro had successfully achieved one of its key objectives: to inform and educate the public on the differences and advantages of privatization over a public fire department.

The city was heartened by the results, particularly since relations with the union firefighters continued to deteriorate. Rural/Metro expected an RFP to be issued the following month. Such was not to be the case. Charges and counter-charges were flying, and more lawsuits and legal claims were being threatened and filed. Contract negotiations broke down completely when the city's labor attorney would not meet union demands and told a union representative to "stick it right in his ear" and walked out of the contract hearings.

The city subsequently charged the union with engaging in an illegal strike for not responding to a general alarm that had occurred in early December. The charge asked that the union be decertified, fined $20,000, and charged for the city's legal costs.

The city continued to delay the release of an RFP and indicated it might wait until after the referendum, which now seemed a certainty to make the ballot for the November 1986 general election. In mid-February 1986 Rural/Metro pulled its representation out of the city. Subsequently legislation was introduced that would have given all municipalities the option to consider privatization as an alternative to public services. Had such a bill been signed into law, it would have effectively nullified the union firefighters' referendum. It did not become law. Instead, it was assigned to a special committee for study. The fact that the firefighters union lobbied against the legislation was more than coincidental to the bill's virtual demise.

The city, continuing its fight, sued the union in an attempt to have the referendum on privatization declared unconstitutional. This effort also failed, and the referendum found its place on the November 1986 general election ballot. A "Yes" vote would mean that the city would lose its option to privatize essential city services. The firefighters union campaigned vigorously to win the referendum, relying heaving upon advertising and door-to-door contacts. Balancing these efforts was a citizens' committee—chaired by the mayor—to keep the privatization issue in proper perspective and, more importantly, to get the vote out to defeat the referendum. The mayor was privatization's most visible and vocal supporter in his efforts to balance the issue before the public. While he never said he favored privatization, he was resolute in his determination to explore the pros and cons and present the issue to the public in a objective manner.

Before the referendum a hearing was held by the State Public Employee Relations Council on the city's strike charges against the union. The judge failed to uphold the charges, even though it was conceded through testimony that the fire department—for the first time in its history—failed to respond to a general alarm. A string of union firefighters had testified that they were either sick, that their paging units did not work, or that the communications alarm system had failed that day.

Still, the private sector saw victory soon after. The referendum failed: privatization won, the city won, and Rural/Metro won. The voters overwhelmingly supported the city's right to retain the option to contract with the private sector. The city carried all five precincts. It was clearly a victory for the city, for privatization, and partially for Rural/Metro as a privatization pioneer.

It had a very sobering effect on the firefighters. With virtually no discussion, no dissension, and no demands, they eagerly signed a new contract with the city, a contract that was far less generous than what they could have had in the first place, reducing benefits and implementing a merit pay system for firefighters.

Rural/Metro would not see a Request for Proposal. The city and the union went through a healing process, licking wounds and mending fences. But there can be little doubt that the city benefited from the efforts of Rural/Metro. The city was sincere in its initial efforts to look at privatization as a viable option to a traditional municipal emergency service.

The privatization issue was also the most expensive political issue in the city's history and in the thirty-nine-year history of Rural/Metro. Nevertheless, Rural/Metro President Ron Butler concluded that, even though the company may have won a battle and lost the war, it was a battle worth fighting, not only for Rural/Metro but for privatization.

In conclusion, Rural/Metro will remain very active in the privatization arena and continue its growth and development in the emergency services field. Municipal governments and enlightened citizens and taxpayers understand the cost-effective benefits and increased productivity that privatization has demonstrated over the years in many areas that were traditionally government operated. Rural/Metro, celebrating forty years of excellence, is proud to be a role model for privatization and a leader in developing increased privatization opportunities. Privatization has certainly arrived, and it is not about to go away.

8

American Health Care and the Economics of Change

C. WAYNE HIGGINS

THE EVOLUTION OF HEALTH POLICY

The health service industry today is undergoing the most rapid and dramatic restructuring in its history. These changes are creating new financing and delivery systems and new relationships between providers and payers. This chapter discusses current changes and future trends. First, however, it is necessary to put these changes in a historical context by reviewing the evolution of health policy in the United States during the postwar era.

The Era of Expansion

By the end of World War II, third-party financing for medical care had emerged in the United States. The Blue Cross plans, which were developed by the hospital industry during the Great Depression, set the pattern for private hospital insurance. They featured service benefits, community rating, free choice of provider, individual payment rates for hospitals (later to evolve into cost-based reimbursement), and no cost controls. Commercial insurers entered the health insurance market during the war as health benefits began to be offered by large employers. They could compete with the Blue Cross plans by offering experience-rated group indemnity policies with benefits tailored to the needs of the employer. However, their small market share prevented them from implementing cost controls that constrained provider prices.

This system of employment-centered private health insurance received considerable impetus when the U.S. Supreme Court ruled that health benefits were subject to collective bargainng and the Internal Revenue Service exempted employer contributions for employee health benefits from the tax base. This tax subsidy made health insurance significantly cheaper for persons able to obtain coverage through their employers and contributed to the rapid expansion of private health insurance during the 1950s. In 1950, private health insurance paid 29.3 percent of the net cost of nonfederal, short-stay hospitals while direct consumer payments accounted for 49.5 percent. By 1960, insurance was paying 52.5 percent and consumers were paying only 28.7 percent out of pocket (Eastaugh, 1981: 5).

Unfortunately, the federally subsidized private health insurance system contained a number of flaws. First, only persons obtaining coverage from their employers could use the tax loophole. Self-employed and unemployed persons had to buy insurance with after-tax dollars. Second, large unionized employers typically offered generous health benefits and could obtain favorable premiums, but small employers faced higher premiums and typically offered limited benefits or none at all. Thus, even among the employed population, coverage was uneven and for some, nonexistent. Third, the tax expenditure was both regressive and expensive. The exemption is worth more to persons in higher marginal tax brackets, and its cost to the treasury is uncontrollable, rising along with the cost of health insurance. By 1980 federal tax expenditures for health insurance equaled $10.6 billion (Greenspan and Vogel, 1980). Finally, the elderly and the poor were excluded from employment-based coverage, and most were unable to afford expensive individual policies. Thus, large segments of the population remained uninsured while the growth in insurance fueled inflation in medical costs. This created political pressure for government relief which resulted in the enactment of Medicare and Medicaid in 1965.

Medicare, Title XVII, and Medicaid, Title XIX, of the Social Security Amendments of 1965 were the most expansionary federal health programs ever enacted. They provided government health insurance to the elderly (Title XVII) and the poor (Title XIX) and a substantial infusion of public funds into the hospital industry. Unfortunately, they adopted the open-ended, inflationary reimbursement system (cost-based reimbursement for hospitals and fee-for-service payment for physicians) that had evolved in the private sector. Neither program incorporated cost controls when first implemented. The impact of these programs on health care costs was immediate and dramatic. Health care costs, which were increasing at an annual rate of 8.6 percent in 1965, jumped to 12.1 percent in 1967 (the first full year under Medicare) and remained in double digits for almost twenty years (Feldstein, 1983: 2). The hospital industry was a major benefactor of the new programs. Liberal definitions of cost and generous depreciation schedules provided substantial amounts of investment capital for hospitals. This came at an opportune time for the industry because federal construction funds made available through the Hill-Burton program of 1946 were no longer sufficient to meet the increasing demand for capital (Hyman, 1975). Medicare fueled a construction boom in the hospital industry which lasted into the early 1980s and resulted in excess bed capacity and redundant and underused services and technology (Cromwell et al., 1987).

Medicare also gave rise to the investor-owned hospital corporation. Proprietary hospital chains emerged shortly after the enactment of Medicare (the first appeared in 1968) and developed rapidly. During the 1970s the for-profit hospital industry grew faster than the computer industry, experiencing a 68 percent growth in beds between 1976 and 1981 (Starr, 1982: 430). Proprietary chains posed competitive challenges to voluntary hospitals, which responded by establishing nonprofit hospital corporations and alliances. This joint development of for-profit and not-for-profit multihospital systems heralded the first modern restructuring of the health care system, the horizontal integration of the hospital industry. By 1980 an American Hospital Association survey found 245 multihospital systems operating 301,894 beds (about 30 percent of all community hospital beds). Nonprofit systems operated 57.6 percent of these beds while investor-owned corporations operated 35.1 percent and public systems (excluding federal) operated 7.3 percent.

Other expansionary federal policies addressed medical manpower, especially the supply of physicians. Reforms undertaken in the wake of the Flexner Report of 1910 had resulted in the closing of more than half of the nation's medical schools (from 162 in 1906 to 69 in 1944), state licensure for physicians, accreditation for medical schools, and a decline in the physician-to-population ratio. During the 1960s and 1970s the federal government responded to a perceived physician shortage by subsidizing medical education, expanding U.S. medical schools, and making it easier for foreign-trained physicians to immigrate. The result has been a dramatic growth in the physician supply. Today, the United States is experiencing a physician surplus, which is expected to increase significantly in the coming decade (Ginzberg and Ostow, 1984).

The major emphasis of federal health policy during the era of expansion was improving access and quality. In addition to the expansion of hospital and physician resources, substantial public investments were made in allied health education, nursing education, and biomedical research. The result was a golden era in American medicine, when hospitals flourished, physicians' incomes soared, new technology and therapies proliferated, and the majority of the public enjoyed greater access to steadily improving care.

The two major shortcomings of expansionary policies were their failure to contain costs and their contribution to serious resource misallocations. High and sustained medical cost inflation ultimately brought an end to expansionary policies as government found it increasingly difficult to fund health entitlements and private employers became alarmed over rising health insurance premiums.

Expansionary programs also failed to create a balanced and cost-effective delivery system. The postwar infusion of public and private dollars resulted in an overbuilt and costly hospital industry and an overemphasis on high-technology, specialized medicine. More cost-effective, preventive, ambulatory, and primary care services were underdeveloped because they were largely excluded from the third-party reimbursement system (Fuchs, 1974).

The Era of Regulation

Soaring Medicare and Medicaid costs forced government to intervene in the health care industry by implementing a series of command and control regulations. During the 1970s these regulations coexisted with expansionary reimbursement programs as government attempted to pursue improved access and cost containment simultaneously. During this period, extending from the mid-1960s to the early 1980s, government enacted three distinct forms of regulation: investment controls, utilization controls, and price controls.

State certificate-of-need (CON) regulations are the primary investment controls. The federal government implemented a similar regulation under Section 1122 of the Social Security Amendments of 1972 (P.L. 93-603), but it has had less impact than CON. Certificate-of-need programs vary from state to state, but generally these programs require institutional providers (hospitals and nursing homes) to obtain permission from state governments before making capital investments above a given threshold (originally $100,000), increasing bed supply, or adding new services. The economic justification for CON is the belief that excess capacity in the hospital industry increases costs and encourages unnecessary hospitalization.

Studies that found that much of the increase in hospital costs that took place during the 1970s was attributable to increased service intensity (more tests and treatments per admission) cast doubt on the ability of CON to restrain costs significantly (Gibson and Fisher, 1977; Russell, 1979; Feldstein, 1977). Other researchers have concluded that CON caused hospitals to invest less in bed expansion and more in technology (Salkever and Bice, 1979) and that stimulated increased labor inputs (Sloan and Steinwald, 1978). National trends in hospital costs during the 1970s suggest little or no effect on overall costs.

Ultilization controls for Medicare and Medicaid patients were enacted under the provisions of Title XI of the Social Security Amendments of 1972. This program organized a nationwide network of Professional Standards Review Organizations (PSRO's) to monitor quality and prevent unnecessary hospitalization. These organizations were physician controlled and used concurrent review of hospital charts as their principal cost-control method. Under concurrent review, a representative of the PSRO reviewed patient charts and determined whether treatments and length of stay (LOS) were consistent with norms for similar patients with the same diagnosis. If the LOS was determined to be excessive or tests and treatments unnecessary, Medicare reimbursement could be terminated.

In 1979 the Health Care Financing Administration (HCFA) published an evaluation of the PSRO program. Its principal findings were that PSRO had generated only small savings over administrative costs ($5 million in 1977 and $21 million in 1978) and that the program's effects were not uniform across the nation (Health Care Financing Administration, 1979). These results were not surprising, given that the first few days of a hospital admission are the most expensive (most diagnostic tests and treatments occur early) and that concurrent review focused on shortening hospital stays rather than preventing unnecessary hospitalizations. The PSRO program has been replaced by a similar but stronger utilization control program in conjunction with the Medicare Prospective Payment System (PPS).

Price controls were applied to the hospital industry in some states in the form of prospective rate regulation (PR). These programs were introduced in New Jersey (1969) and New York (1970) and had been adopted in twenty-seven states by 1978. Programs varied in several dimensions, notably their statutory authority (some were mandatory, some were voluntary), the unit of payment controlled (some controlled total budgets, some daily room rates) and the number of participating payers (some regulated only Medicaid payments, some only Blue Cross, others most or all payers including Medicare). All programs were based on the public utility model of regulation, which assumes that the regulated industry is experiencing market failure and that government must regulate price in order to protect the public interest. Hospitals were viewed as monopolistic because they experienced little price competition, their product was heterogeneous, their consumers were poorly informed, and entry into supply side of the market was restricted (Bailey, 1977).

Studies evaluating the effects of PR found that mandatory programs were modestly successful in restraining hospital price inflation. Reimbursement limits were shown to have reduced the rate of growth in expenditures by approximately 3 to 5 percentage points when compared to states without PR (Sloan, 1981; Coelen and Sullivan, 1981; Congressional Budget Office, 1979; General Accounting Office, 1980).

Despite the limited success of some state PR programs, command and control regulation generally failed to control health cost inflation. This led to a fundamental change in federal health policy in the 1980s when indirect regulation and competition became the preferred instruments of cost control.

Direct regulation failed because it did not address the major cause of health cost inflation—the perverse incentives of the open-ended system of third-party payment. Figure 8.1 presents a demand-pull model of health cost inflation described by Eastaugh (1981: 3-24) and illustrates the point at which direct regulations were applied. In this model, the growth of private insurance and later the introduction of Medicare and Medicaid provided patients with progressively greater insurance coverage. Because most medical care is elective (the timing of its use is under the control of the patient) and because significant moral hazard exists with health insurance (having insurance increases the use of elective services), more insurance resulted in greater demand for care and less

Figure 8.1
The Demand-Pull Inflation and Direct Regulation of the 1970s

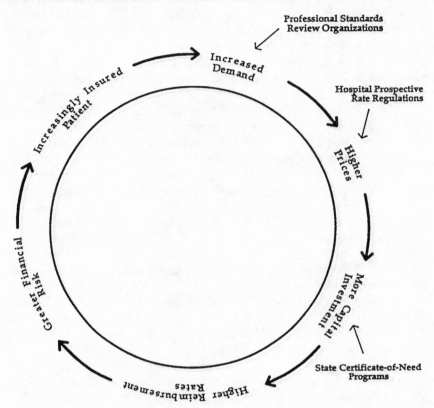

sensitivity to price. This created an environment of excess demand wherein providers could easily raise prices. Higher prices encouraged greater capital investment, especially in hospitals. Under cost-based reimbursement increased capitalization automatically led to higher reimbursement rates. This translated into higher insurance premiums and out-of-pocket expenses as these costs were passed through to the public. Finally, higher out-of-pocket costs caused the public to demand more comprehensive insurance coverage in an increasing cycle of greater subsidy and higher price.

Investment regulation attempted to control capital spending while the reimbursement system encouraged greater investment. Utilization controls sought to limit hospital use in the face of insurance that paid a much larger percentage for inpatient care than for equivalent outpatient services. And price controls enjoyed only modest success in a few states by directly controlling hospital budgets. These regulations were in direct opposition to the incentives of the reimbursement system which encouraged greater resource consumption and capital investment in hospitals. Not surprisingly the incentives of third-party reimbursement prevailed, thus setting the stage for a policy shift that triggered the dramatic changes now taking place.

AN ECONOMIC TRANSORMATION?

Two events contributed to the shift in health policy since 1980. First, the election of President Ronald Reagan, a conservative dedicated to free-market principles, meant that command and control regulation was philosophically incompatible with the economic preferences of the administration. Second, the recession of the early 1980s forced business and industry to formulate private sector responses to rising medical costs.

Medicare Reform

The Medicare Prospective Payment System (PPS), which became operational in 1984, changes hospital reimbursement under Medicare Part A from a cost-based retrospective payment system to one in which payment is determined in advance on the basis of diagnosis and treatment (Smits et al., 1984). Two aspects of the PPS are significant: It pays hospitals on the basis of the admission rather than on specific units of treatment (bundling), and it determines the amount of payment for cases of similar types from a schedule published prior to treatment (prospective payment). Prospective payment by the case creates incentives to minimize inputs per admission and length of stay (LOS). It also encourages hospitals to determine their average and marginal costs of treating patients in each of the 468 diagnosis related groups (DRG's) in order to identify and control excessive costs.

The major limitations of the PPS are its potential to biased treatment decisions (Omenn and Conrad, 1984; Relman, 1985), influence on the selection of patients and the offering of services by hospitals (Jencks et al., 1984), and its vulnerability to "gaming" (Stern and Epstein, 1985). The first three problems arise if the case classification system is inaccurate and/or if the payment schedule systematically over or underpays for some DRG's. Since the implementation of PPS there have been charges that hospitals are discharging patients prematurely, dumping high-cost patients, and putting unjustified pressure on physicians to minimize treatment costs and LOS for Medicare patients.

The fact that the PPS entails incentives to undertreat and is vulnerable to gaming in the form of misclassification of diagnosis and premature discharge and readmission required that a watchdog utilization review program be established. This led to the development of Peer Review Organizations (PRO's), successors to the PSRO's of the 1970s. Like their predecessors, PRO's are charged with the responsibility of preventing unnecessary hospitalization and monitoring quality of care. However, the new organizations rely primarily on prior authorization for elective admissions, rather than concurrent review to control utilization. Under prior authorization, a physician must receive PRO approval to admit a Medicare patient for elective treatment. If the PRO determines that the care should be rendered in an outpatient setting, it will not authorize payment for inpatient care. This regulation offers the potential for greater savings than concurrent review, because the whole admission rather than the last few days of care can be avoided. PRO's are also charged with validating patient diagnosis and DRG assignment (to prevent the deliberate misclassification of patients into higher-paying DRG's) and with the review of all readmissions occurring within two weeks of discharge (to prevent double payment through premature discharge and readmission).

The coming of PPS/PRO represented a shift in federal health policy from an emphasis on direct, command and control regulation to indirect, incentive-based regulation (PPS) supported by direct regulation (PRO). The new payment system also heralded a shift from trying to control total system costs to controlling only federal costs and forcing state governments and private industry to fend for themselves.

Prospective payment has helped slow the rate of inflation in hospital costs. Table 8.1 reveals annual percent change in selected components of the Consumer Price Index (CPI) between 1970 and 1986. Note that beginning in 1985, price increases for all hospital rooms, which had historically risen faster than prices for all medical care combined, dropped below the all-item index. By 1986, hospital room charges were increasing at a rate below physician service price increases. This slowing of hospital cost inflation reduced Medicare Part A outlays and pushed back by several years the date at which the Hospital Insurance Trust Fund is projected to become insolvent.

It should be noted, however, that medical costs relative to general price inflation have accelerated during the 1980s. During the 1970-1975 interval, medical care prices increased only 0.2 percent faster than the CPI. Between 1975 and 1980 they increased 0.6 percent faster. However, for the five years between 1982 and 1986 medical care prices increased 4.2 percent faster than the CPI. Even when declining energy prices are omitted, medical care prices increased 3.5 percent faster than general inflation. This has serious implications for future health policy, which will be discussed in the last section.

In part the limited success of the PPS in controlling hospital costs and the high real inflation in general medical costs illustrates the limitations of a fragmented approach to cost containment. Reduced expenditures in one treatment setting are not net savings because they are partially offset by higher expenditures in others. Thus, some of the Medicare Part A (hospital inpatient) savings resulting from prospective payment have been offset by higher Medicare Part B (outpatient) expenditures as care that would otherwise have occurred in hospitals is performed on an outpatient basis. Likewise, the savings of one payer (Medicare) can result in higher expenditures for other payers as hospitals cost shift to regain lost revenues (Ginsburg and Sloan, 1984).

Table 8.1

Annual Percent Change in Selected Components of the Consumer Price Index for All Urban Consumers, 1970-1986

Item	1970-75	1975-80	1981	1982	1983	1984	1985	1986
			Annual percent change					
All items	6.7	8.9	10.4	6.1	3.2	4.3	3.6	1.9
All itmes less energy	6.5	8.2	10.0	6.7	3.6	4.7	3.9	3.9
Medical care	6.9	9.5	10.8	11.6	8.7	6.2	6.2	7.5
Medical care services	7.6	9.9	10.7	11.9	8.7	6.0	6.0	7.7
Physician services	6.9	9.7	11.0	9.4	7.7	7.0	5.8	7.2
Hospital and other medical services*	--	--	14.2	14.2	11.4	8.6	6.4	6.0
Hospital room	10.2	12.2	14.8	15.7	11.3	8.3	5.9	6.0
Prescription drugs	1.6	7.2	11.4	11.7	10.9	9.6	9.5	8.6
All items less medical care	6.7	8.8	10.3	5.9	2.9	4.1	3.4	1.5
Housing	6.8	9.9	11.5	7.2	2.7	4.1	4.0	2.9
Food and beverages	8.4	7.6	7.8	4.1	2.2	3.8	2.3	3.2
Transportation	6.0	10.6	12.1	4.1	2.4	4.5	2.6	-3.9

*Not available prior to December 1977

SOURCE: Bureau of Labor Statistics: Data from the Consumer Price Index Program. Detailed CPI report. Washington, D.C., U.S. Government Printing Office, various issues in 1986 and 1987.

Medicaid Reform

The Omnibus Budget Reconciliation Act (OBRA) of 1981 allowed states greater flexibility in operating their Medicaid programs. The most important change permits states to waive the free-choice-of-provider requirement and lock Medicaid patients into managed, at-risk health care systems. Case management implies that utilization is monitored and controlled, usually by a primary care physician. At-risk contracting requires that providers assume some or all of the financial risk associated with medical care utilization. Both requirements create incentives to minimize inpatient hospital care, especially marginal and unnecessary care. The most common form of case-management system is the Primary Care Network (PCN), in which a closed panel of primary care physicians contracts with the state government to provide primary and manage referral and inpatient care for Medicaid beneficiaries within a given geographical area. Payment is usually on a capitation basis with penalties levied if costs exceed a target level.

States lost no time in establishing these systems. By March 1983 twenty-nine states had applied for waivers permitting case management and ten states had operational systems (Sullivan and Gibson, 1983). The principal economic effect of PCN's is to promote competition among providers through the contracting/competitive-bidding process and by "locking up" large numbers of patients who are no longer available to fee-for-service (FFS) medicine. They also promote hospital competition through discounts for PCN business, and because most PCN's incorporate incentives to decrease inpatient utilization.

Evidence to date suggests that PCN's are easiest to organize in metropolitan areas that have a surplus of physicians and hospital beds. They do not lend themselves to sparsely populated and underserved areas (Freund and Neuschler, 1986). States have also contracted with health maintenance organizations (HMO's) and health insuring organizations (HIO's) under the provisions of OBRA. Both types of organizations are paid on a fully capitated basis and seek to control costs primarily by avoiding unnecessary inpatient hospital care.

Private Sector Reform

Four significant trends underlie cost control reforms in the private sector: the changing role of employers from passive payers to prudent buyers, the transformation of the health insurance industry from a risk-sharing system into a service industry, the growth of managed health care, and the vertical integration of the health care industry.

Employers, who traditionally have been passive payers for medical services, were forced to become prudent purchasers in response to rising medical benefit costs. In 1984 U.S. corporations paid about $90 billion in health insurance premiums. This amounted to 38 percent of pretax profits, more than was paid to shareholders in dividends (Califano, 1986). General Motors saw its health insurance costs increase from $575 million in 1973 (an average of $765 per employee and family) to $2.2 billion in 1983 ($2,897 per employee and family). During this ten-year period health benefit costs increased from 5 percent to 10 percent of employee compensation (Woodall et al., 1987).

During the 1970s medical cost inflation in an era of low productivity growth and increasing international competition forced large employers to self-insure under the provisions of the Employee Retirement Income Security Act of 1974 (ERISA). Under ERISA, self-insured plans are exempt from state insurance regulations, including reserve requirements, mandated benefits, and premium taxes. This gives employers greater flexibility in structuring their benefit packages and allows them to save the costs of taxes and reserves by paying health benefit costs out of operating funds. Total self-insurance, where the employer assumes the entire risk for employee health costs, is implemented only by large employers that can afford unexpectedly high costs. Nonetheless, by 1983, 17.5 percent of the private health insurance market was accounted for by self-insured plans (Arnett and Trapnell, 1984).

Faced with the loss of their largest accounts, insurers sought to recapture this business by offering actuarial support and claims processing through administrative services only (ASO) contracts. Under these arrangements, insurance companies estimate future costs and pay medical bills for self-insured companies but assume no risk for claims cost. The availability of these services allowed the full flowering of self-insurance during the 1980s. A 1987 survey found only 10 percent of employers of various sizes fully insured under pooled risk programs, 26 percent were fully insured under experience-rated programs, 18 percent had minimum premium programs (MPP's), and 46 percent were self-funded, with the carrier providing "administrative services only." For companies with over 40,000 employees, 85 percent were on ASO's, as were virtually all of the Fortune 1,000 (Patricelli, 1987). Minimum premium plans allow medium-sized employers to self-insure partially by providing stop-loss coverage. Employees using MMP's also purchase administrative services. More recently, small employer trusts have allowed smaller employers to capture some of the benefits of self-insurance by pooling several small work forces into a single risk pool and providing stop-loss insurance and administrative services.

Total and partial self-insurance allowed employers to capture savings associated with insurance regulations, profits, and overhead, but these are a small part of the total cost of employee health benefits. To control costs associated with medical prices and utilization, employers have embraced strategies involving information management and private regulation. Information management strategies rely on computer technology and the method of small area analysis developed by John E. Wennberg of the Dartmouth Medical School and Alan Gittelsohn of Johns Hopkins School of Medicine (Caper and Zubkoff, 1984).

Small area analysis is a population-based analysis of medical practice patterns in a given geographical area, usually a city or a health service catchment area. This type of analysis compares local practice patterns to national and state data and across individual providers. The results can reveal patterns of overservice, such as excessive hysterectomy rates and/or inefficient delivery patterns among physicians and hospitals. These results can be used to educate providers in an attempt to modify practice habits and improve outcomes or to steer employees toward more effective and efficient doctors and hospitals. Employers can accomplish the latter by sharing cost and outcome data with employees needing specific treatments, especially elective surgery.

Small area analysis can be conducted by large employers, government planning agencies, or health coalitions (voluntary organizations composed of employers, representatives of the hospital and health insurance industries, and in some cases representatives of local medical societies). Health coalitions have become increasingly popular in recent years, and information sharing is one of their principal functions.

Private regulation involves employers adding provisions to their health benefits packages which impact on the delivery of medical services. An early example is the requirement that employees seek second opinions when elective surgery is recommended. In roughly one-third of the cases, a second opinion fails to confirm the original recommendation. Employees are usually free to choose whether or not to undergo the procedure regardless of the second opinion, and some programs will pay for a third opinion when there is disagreement. A more stringent form of private regulation is concurrent review of inpatient hospital care. This review is similar to that which PSRP provided for Medicare patients (some employers contracted with PSRO's to review employee records). Concurrent review seeks to reduce inpatient hospital care by promoting early discharge. In recent years, a similar review has been conducted retrospectively on the records of discharged patients with payment being denied for care deemed unnecessary (both PRO's and some private utilization companies conduct these reviews).

Currently the most popular and most effective form of private regulation is prior approval screens. Prior approval screening is a generic cost-control method widely practiced by HMO's, PPO's, and now traditional insurance plans. Vendors of this service estimate that about 35 percent of the employer market now use hospital prior approval screens supplied either by insurance carriers or by about fifty independent utilization review companies. These screens can result in a 15 to 20 percent reduction in bed days and a 5 to 10 percent savings in claim costs (Patricelli, 1987). Prior approval can also help identify potentially high-cost cases before hospitalization, so that a case manager can be assigned to coordinate the entire course of treatment from hospitalization to postdischarge care. Since 3 percent of cases account for 50 percent of claims cost, identifying these patients and managing their care has the potential for substantial savings.

Employers are also using case management in specialty areas such as mental health, substance abuse, and dental services. Specialized utilization review in these areas applies the same techniques (prior authorization for elective procedures) used in the medical/surgical area.

Today, many employers have been forced to abandon their historic role as passive payer for medical services and assume the more assertive posture of prudent buyer and private regulator. To date, however, their impact has been limited because their immense economic power has not been fully employed.

With existing information management systems the potential for private regulation of health care is substantial, especially if employers share information and coordinate their actions on a regional basis. It should also be noted that employers have increased employee coinsurance rates and deductibles, created incentive plans which discourage unnecessary utilization, and allowed employees to choose among various fringe benefit options (cafeteria plans). These actions have largely stopped the postwar trend toward more comprehensive health insurance for large segments of the public.

The health insurance industry is being transformed by the need to develop new insurance products and insurance-related services, adopt new technology, and accommodate employer demands for cost containment. The growth of self-insurance has meant declining demand for traditional insurance products and growing demand for insurance-related servies such as ASO's and utilization review. This is changing the health insurance industry from a risk-sharing mechanism into a service industry (Higgins and Meyers, 1987). This process started in the mid-1960s when insurance companies were awarded contracts to act as Medicare fiscal intermediaries and accelerated in response to employer self-insurance.

Today, most health insurance claims are handled on paper. However, current technology offers the potential for processing claims faster and at lower cost through electronic claims submission, editing, and processing (Etheredge, 1986). Electronic billing avoids labor-intensive paper claims processing and is already in use by some large firms, such as Electronic Data Systems, a subsidiary of General Motors, and National Electronic Information Corporation. To maximize the potential for electronic billing, providers and claims processors must be linked through computer networks. The capital costs of installing such systems could be prohibitive for insurers commanding small market shares. It may also prove impractical for individual providers to be linked to several billing systems simultaneously.

Despite these limitations, electronic billing will almost certainly grow because it offers substantial savings in claims processing costs. However, in so doing, these systems are likely to contribute to consolidation in the health insurance industry as those firms with sufficient market share to justify the investment develop electronic billing and gain a cost advantage over their smaller competitors. Today, in many large states 300 or more health insurance companies compete for business and, with the exception of Blue Cross and Blue Shield, few have even a 5 percent market share (Etheridge, 1986). Low market share can impede the ability of insurers to negotiate discounts and utilization controls with providers, establish HMO and PPO networks, and use electronic billing. The most likely result is consolidation as companies with large market share grow at the expense of their competitors.

As a shakeout occurs in the health insurance industry, hospitals and physicians will be confronted by fewer but more powerful and better informed payers. Insurers will use data to select cost-effective providers for insurer-sponsored HMO's and PPO's. In a more concentrated industry, insurers will have both the information to identify cost-effective providers and the clout to force contractual concessions. Their leverage will grow in proportion to enrollment in their health plans. Historically, the fragmented third-party payment system and the competition between payers worked to the advantage of providers because cost-containment efforts by any one payer placed its subscribers or beneficiaries at a disadvantage in obtaining services (Paringler, 1979; Greenspan and Vogel, 1980). However, the unanimous efforts by payers to contain costs and the consolidation of the health insurance industry will weaken the position of providers relative to that of payers. Hospitals will find their destiny increasingly controlled by third-party payers and physicians will find their influence and autonomy reduced.

Managed care refers to systems of health service delivery in which the patients' use of medical services and, in some cases, their choice of provider is restricted. The principal intent of managed care is to avoid unnecessary hospitalization. Recently, managed care systems have sought to identify high-cost patients and closely manage their care both in and out of the hospital. The oldest form of managed care is the HMO. More recently, PPO's and managed indemnity plans have been developed as well.

HMO's have existed in various forms under various names since the turn of the century (Mayer and Mayer, 1985). In the last few years, support from employers, unions, and the federal government has greatly accelerated their growth. By early 1985, there were 350 HMO's enrolling more than 15 million people nationwide, and enrollment was growing at approximately 20 percent per year (Interstudy, 1985). Growth was most rapid among multistate for-profit HMO's as hundreds of millions of dollars in private capital flowed into the industry. Sustained HMO growth is expected, with total revenues for the industry projected to reach $35 billion by 1990 (Masso, 1985).

The growth of HMO's challenges both hospitals and insurers. Hospitals face declining occupancy because group model HMO's use fewer inpatient services than traditionally insured systems (Manning et al., 1984; Enthoven, 1980). Hospitals are also under pressure to compete for HMO contracts by offering discounts. Insurers face the prospect of declining market share for their indemnity and service-benefit products as HMO's offer more favorable benefit and premium packages. To compete, insurers and providers are developing at-risk products such as independent practice associations (IPA's) and preferred provider organizations (PPO's). IPA's, like group model HMO's embody incentives for reduced inpatient utilization and employ utilization controls (Inglehart, 1984).

PPO's, like IPA's and group model HMO's are presently undergoing rapid development. A 1985 survey found that almost 6 million people were eligible to use PPO's and that the number of eligibles had increased fourfold from late 1984 to mid-1985 (Rice et al., 1985). The study also found that utilization controls, aimed at reducing inpatient hospital care, were almost universal among PPOs. PPOs facilitate competition among both providers and insurers. For insurers they provide new products, featuring discounts and utilization controls, that can compete with HMO's, IPA's, and conventional insurance. Hospitals and physicians view PPO's as a mechanism for protecting and expanding market share and as a means of competing against HMO's.

While PPO's have been developed by hospitals, physician groups, insurers, and entrepreneurs, the insurance industry and hospital corporations are now the leaders in expanding PPO networks. As insurers negotiate PPO contracts with hospitals, the demand for discounts can cause considerable friction. The conflict between Blue Cross and the hospital industry over the Blue's rapidly growing PPO system reflects this divergence of interests between insurers and providers (Powills, 1985).

To compete with HMO's, IPA's, and PPO's while retaining the subscribers' freedom to choose among providers, insurers have developed managed indemnity plans. These plans feature free choice of provider but incorporate case management, usually in the form of prior authorization for elective hospitalization, as a cost control mechanism. The development of PPO's and managed indemnity plans has given rise to the so-called "triple option," which some analysts believe will be the preferred health insurance product of the future.

The triple option refers to HMO, PPO, and managed indemnity products offered in one experience-rated package obtained or managed through a single carrier (Patricelli, 1986). This system allows freedom of choice among health plans for employees and allows the employer to capture savings that are lost when HMO products are purchased from separate vendors. As managed care becomes the dominant product, insurers will compete on the basis of premiums, benefits, and quality (Reinhart, 1986). Offering competitive premium/benefit packages will require strict control of inpatient hospital utilization and controlling quality will require monitoring hospitals and physicians and selectively contracting with each.

Vertical integration is occurring rapidly in the health service industry. Two important factors contributing to this restructuring are the need for hospitals to expand outpatient services as a means of capturing revenues lost because of declining inpatient demand and the need to combine the financing and delivery of medical services in order to offer the triple option. The latter is more important, because it departs from the historical separation of finance from delivery and because it has the potential of fundamentally restructuring the health service industry.

In order to offer the full range of managed care products, providers and insurers are being forced to unite through acquisitions, partnerships, and alliances. This process is changing the health service industry from a provider-controlled cottage industry into a modern corporate structure characterized by vertical and horizontal integration. Horizontal integration began in the hospital and nursing home industries during the 1970s with the development of proprietary chains. It continues today with the growth of nonprofit chains and alliances. Vertical integration is also occurring rapidly as hospital corporations become affiliated with health insurers and acquire ambulatory services and nursing homes. The most important aspect of vertical integration is the bundling of insurance products and service delivery. Patricelli (1986) has identified six basic patterns of organization emerging under the pressure of competition.

1. Insurer-initiated vertical integration. This approach involves insurers developing and distributing integrated prepaid and indemnity policies independently. Companies following this strategy include Blue Cross–Blue Shield, CIGNA, The Travelers, and Prudential.

2. Hospital-initiated integration. This strategy involves hospital chains developing or acquiring the ability to offer prepaid and indemnity products. Currently three of the four largest proprietary hospital chains (Hospital Corporation of America, Humana, and National Medical Enterprises) are pursuing this strategy. American Medical International (AMI) recently abandoned a similar effort after experiencing substantial losses.

3. HMO-initiated vertical integration. Here, HMO's develop or acquire PPO's and managed indemnity plans. Several national HMO chains including Maxicare and United Healthcare are following this approach.

4. Insurer joint ventures. This approach involves joint ventures among insurers to develop HMO's and/or PPO's. This strategy is particularly attractive to small insurers lacking the resources to develop these products independently.

5. Insurer-provider joint ventures. This approach involves joint ventures between insurers and hospital chains. The Aetna–Voluntary Hospital of America (Partners) joint venture and the Equitable–HCA joint venture are two examples. Most of these strategies try quickly to establish a network of HMO's and PPO's to augment the insurer's indemnity products.

6. Insurer–HMO joint ventures. Another new development is joint ventures that unite the insurers' indemnity products with the HMOs' prepaid plans. The Lincoln National joint ventures with U.S. Healthcare, Peak, and Pace are examples of this practice.

Some analysts predict that during the 1990s the majority of the privately insured population will be enrolled in vertically integrated systems offering managed care (Ripps and Werronen, 1986). If price competition among vertically integrated systems emerges and follows the pattern in other industries, one can expect today's partnerships and alliances to evolve into formal corporate structures as less efficient organizational structures lose market share and are forced to merge, sell, or go out of business. The high capital costs associated with electronic billing and developing HMO products may hasten the consolidation. One can envision a mature market of the future dominated by a few dozen large, vertically integrated corporations, selling managed care and operating on a regional or national basis.

If competition and indirect regulation continue to dominate national health policy and cost control remains its primary goal, the corporation may come to dominate tomorrow's health care system. Figure 8.2 illustrates a vertically integrated corporate health care system and contrasts it with the system of independent providers and payers.

Under the old system, the multitude of payers and the separation of payment from service delivery complicated cost containment. Each provider, whether local hospital corporation or solo practice physician, was both a cost center and a profit center. Each made investment decisions independently and was under no pressure to consider opportunity costs or societal needs. Quality assurance and liability coverage were the responsibility of each provider. Under this system, physicians dominated because they directed the utilization of virtually all health care resources and controlled the hospitals' access to patients.

A vertically integrated corporation would incorporate different incentives and require different relationships among the principal actors. The corporation would be controlled by an integrated management with responsibility for both insurance products and all levels of service delivery. Most of the corporation's resources would be generated through the sale of insurance products while all clinical services would be cost centers, with hospital inpatient services being the leading one. In a price-competitive environment where multiple health care corporations vie for employer group contracts one would expect that most or all insurance products would shift financial risk to the insurer and that capitated health plans such as HMO's and IPA's would become the dominant insurance products.

As in all businesses, financial risk will require strong management. In the vertically integrated health care corporation, the manager will replace the physician as the dominant actor. This is already happening in hospitals partly in response to the Medicare PPS (Omenn and Conrad, 1984; Relman, 1985; Jencks et al., 1984). In the future, managerial power can be expected to grow roughly in proportion to the size of the corporation and the intensity of the competition it faces. The physician glut, which makes physicians easily replaceable, is already weakening their traditional power.

Investment decisions in the corporation should result in less excess hospital capacity and a more balanced mix of services than has evolved under fee for service. This will occur because the vertically integrated health care corporation will face strong incentives to eliminate excess hospital inpatient capacity (the highest cost center) and develop outpatient and long-term care services that can be substituted for some inpatient care. Corporate managers will have an incentive to consider alternative investments across all products and levels of care when allocating scarce investment capital. Thus, opportunity costs, which today are largely ignored in the decisions of private physicians and individual hospitals will be considered across treatment settings and between services. A likely result will be reduced investment in expensive, high-technology inpatient services and increased investment in primary care,

Figure 8.2
The Vertically Integrated Health Care Corporation and the System of Independent
Payers and Providers

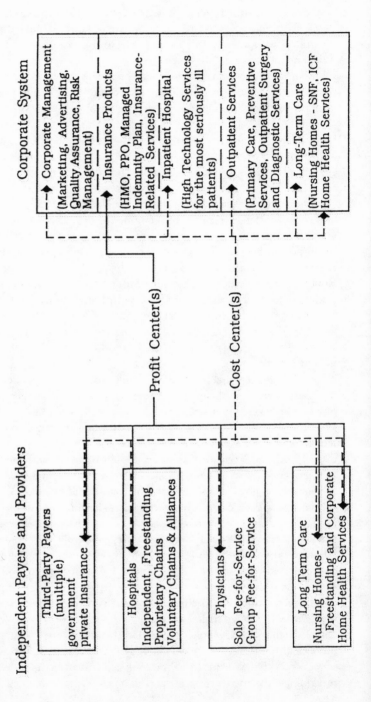

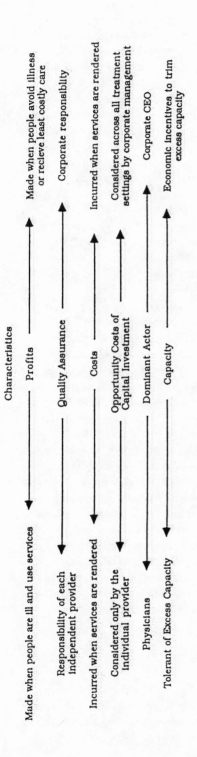

Characteristics

Profits — Made when people are ill and use services / Made when people avoid illness or recieve least costly care

Quality Assurance — Responsibility of each independent provider / Corporate responsiblity

Costs — Incurred when services are rendered / Incurred when services are rendered

Opportunity Costs of Capital Investment — Considered only by the individual provider / Considered across all treatment settings by corporate management

Dominant Actor — Physicians / Corporate CEO

Capacity — Tolerant of Excess Capacity / Economic incentives to trim excess capacity

111

ambulatory diagnostics and surgery, and preventive services. Such a shift in resources would help address some of today's more serious misallocations.

Current trends suggest that competition among health plans will be based on price, convenience, and quality at least insofar as the latter can be accurately measured (Taylor and Kagay, 1986). If medicine comes to be dominated by competing corporations, quality assurance will be an important function. Computer technology is already having a substantial impact on the health care system, and risk management/quality assurance lends itself to this technology. Information systems that combine financial and clinical data will allow managers to profile individual services, facilities, or physicians with respect to resource consumption, case mix, and quality. This information will enable quality assurance and risk management to make comparisons and identify problems throughout the system from the corporate office. This data can be employed in support of selective hiring and contracting by identifying the most cost-effective physicians and facilities. Over time, the use of information systems for monitoring clinical treatments and outcomes should promote a more normative style of medicine as treatments with the highest statistical probability of success become the accepted standard of care.

Price and quality competition among health care corporations could lead them to form closed medical panels in an effort to gain an advantage by employing the most cost-effective physicians. Such a move could lead to more salaried doctors. For physicians whose practice styles or medical outcomes are unacceptable to the corporations, the growth of corporate medicine has ominous implications. These doctors will be forced to compete for the shrinking pool of patients covered by insurance featuring free choice of provider.

The vertically integrated corporation could have even more serious implications for hospitals. Today the nation has a substantial excess of hospital capacity. Health care corporations whose profits are derived from at-risk insurance products will have strong incentives to reduce costs by operating only the minimum necessary level of inpatient hospital capacity (Higgins and Meyers, 1987). Hospitals are already giving discounts in order to obtain HMO and PPO contracts, and proprietary hospital corporations are selling hospitals to free capital for more profitable investments. If vertically integrated corporations evolve from the insurer-provider partnerships of today, they can be expected to operate fewer hospital beds than the present system. The obvious implication is a contraction of the hospital sector as facilities are forced to close, merge or convert.

Policy Considerations

The vertically integrated corporation would pose certain problems, and its coming is not inevitable. The most serious problems presented by these systems are the potential for competition through favorable selection and incentives to undertreat. Any at-risk payment system entails incentives to undertreat. This concern has been raised with regard to both HMO's and the Medicare PPS (Enthoven, 1980; Jencks et al., 1984). Today it is assumed that because a significant amount of health care is reimbursed under fee for service with its incentives to overtreat and because fee-for-service medicine sets the standards of care (including the standards applied in malpractice lawsuits), under-treatment is not a serious problem. This could change, however, when at-risk managed insurance products become dominant. The apparent solutions to this problem include quality competition, with outcome data being widely advertised, and government regulation to deter undertreatment.

At-risk health plans entail incentives to avoid high-risk individuals because a small percentage of seriously ill patients account for a large percentage of health care costs in any risk pool. When at-risk health plans are sold to individuals, the opportunity to compete on the basis of favorable selection becomes a serious concern (Enthoven, 1980). This problem is substantially reduced when health plans are experience-rated and sold to employer groups. And if large numbers of individual policies are anticipated (for example, if Medicare converted to a voucher plan allowing beneficiaries to purchase coverage from competing private vendors), mandatory open enrollment periods and government regulation could be employed. Enthoven (1980: 126-127) has described a system to control favorable selection among competing community-rated health plans.

Figure 8.3 illustrates current reforms in relation to the demand-pull model of medical cost inflation. As previously noted, these changes represent a mix of market competition and regulation. Some innovations are continuing to evolve and grow (for example, managed care and vertically integrated systems), so that it is premature to judge their full economic significance. Nevertheless, the results to date suggest that more drastic restructuring will be required to control health cost inflation (see Table 8.1).

Economists observe that there is no optimal level of health care spending and that society can elect to devote whatever share of its total resources to medical care it chooses. Although this is theoretically true, efforts to reduce the federal budget deficit and enhance international competitiveness will almost certainly require limiting the percentage of national wealth devoted to medical care. Table 8.2 displays aggregate and per capita health expenditures by source of funds for select years between 1980 and 2000. Note that the percentage of total personal health expenditures paid through Medicare is projected to increase from 18 percent in 1987 to almost 23 percent in the year 2000. In dollar terms this translates into an increase in program costs from $78.9 billion to $320.8 billion. The sheer magnitude of federal health expenditures and their rapid rate of growth requires that serious budget reduction measures include further Medicare reforms.

It is also likely that factors related to general economic competitiveness will create pressures to control health costs. In recent years the national economy

Figure 8.3
The Demand-Pull Inflation and Cost-Containment Measures of the 1980s

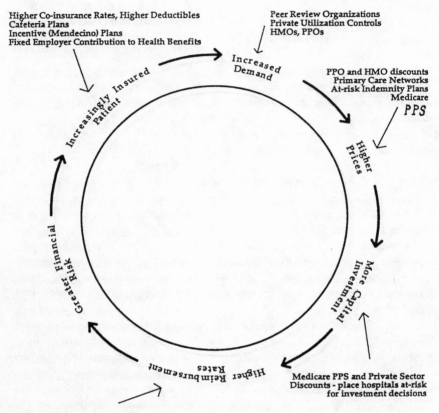

has become more competitive, and one result of increased competition is employer resistance to higher labor costs (Farber, 1987). For more than a decade, health benefit costs have been the most rapidly rising component of total labor costs (Schick, 1987). Because business and industry pays for roughly 30 percent of all personal health expenditures through employee health benefit plans (and helps to support government health programs through corporate taxes), higher medical expenditures lead directly to higher prices for domestically produced goods and services.

Table 8.3 displays selected health status indicators and the percentage of the Gross Domestic Product (GDP) devoted to health expenditures for the United States and its principal Organization for Economic Cooperation and

Table 8.2
Personal Health Care Expenditures Aggregate, Per Capita Amounts and Percent Distribution (by Source of Funds), Selected Calendar Years 1980-2000

Year	Total	Direct patient payments	All third parties	Private health insurance	Other private funds	Third parties Total	Government Federal	Government State and local	Government Medicare	Government Medicaid
1980	$219.7	$63.0	$156.7	$67.5	$2.7	$86.5	$62.5	$24.0	$35.7	$25.2
1987	438.9	127.9	311.0	136.0	5.5	169.6	128.8	40.8	78.9	47.5
1990	573.5	162.0	411.5	175.4	7.2	228.9	178.2	50.7	113.5	61.1
1995	900.5	249.1	651.4	271.5	11.9	368.0	294.9	73.2	197.0	91.5
2000	1,398.1	386.1	1,012.0	417.5	19.4	575.2	468.8	106.4	320.8	138.0
				Per capita amount						
1980	$934	$268	$666	$287	$11	$367	$266	$102	(3)	(3)
1987	1,744	508	1,236	540	22	674	512	162	(3)	(3)
1990	2,225	628	1,596	680	28	888	691	197	(3)	(3)
1995	3,371	933	2,438	1,016	45	1,377	1,104	274	(3)	(3)
2000	5,075	1,401	3,674	1,515	70	2,088	1,702	386	(3)	(3)
				Percent distribution						
1980	100.0	28.7	71.3	30.7	1.2	39.4	28.4	10.9	16.2	11.5
1987	100.0	29.1	70.9	31.0	1.2	38.6	29.3	9.3	18.0	10.8
1990	100.0	28.2	71.8	30.6	1.3	39.9	31.1	8.8	19.8	10.6
1995	100.0	27.7	72.3	30.1	1.3	40.9	32.7	8.1	21.9	10.2
2000	100.0	27.6	72.4	29.9	1.4	41.1	33.5	7.6	22.9	9.9

Subset of Federal funds

Subset of Federal and State and local funds

Calculation of per capita estimates is inappropriate

SOURCE: Health Care Financing Administration

Table 8.3

Selected Health Status Indicators and Health Expenditures as Percentage of Gross Domestic Product for United States and Select Members of the Organization for Economic Cooperation and Development, 1980s

Country	Male Life Expectancy (yr) at birth	Female life expectancy at birth	Infant Deaths per 1,000 live births male (yr)	Infant Death per 1,00 live births female	Percent GDP devoted to health expenditures in 1983
Canada	72.0 (82)	79.0	10.4 (82)	7.8	8.7
Japan	74.8 (84)	80.7	6.6 (84)	5.6	6.7
W. Germany	71.3 (84)	78.1	10.6 (84)	8.9	8.2
United Kingdom	71.3 (82)	77.3	12.2 (82)	9.4	6.2
France	70.9 (81)	79.1	11.2 (81)	8.2	9.3
United States	70.9 (82)	78.4	12.8 (82)	10.2	10.8
OECD Average	71.0	77.7	11.6	9.4	9.6

Source: Organization for Economic Cooperation and Development, Financing and Delivering Health Care (Paris Fr. OECD, 1987) and

Measuring Health Care: 1960–1983 (Paris Fr. OECD, 1985) Various tables in each

Development (OECD) trading partners. It is apparent that the United States outspends its competitors for medical services, but these expenditures do not translate into a healthier population. This observation is consistent with a substantial body of literature indicating that the leading causes of death and disability in developed nations are behavior related (Matarazzo et al., 1984) and that remedial medicine has a limited ability to alter the consequences of chronic disease (Fuchs, 1974; Dever, 1980).

Significantly higher health spending that does not contribute to a healthier, more productive population is detrimental to international competitiveness in two ways. First, it results in higher production cost because of the impact of employee health benefit costs. Second, resources committed to health care are unavailable for investment in education, basic and applied research, and the purchase of new plant and equipment, all important contributors to a nation's competitiveness. It seems likely, therefore, that as the domestic economy becomes increasingly exposed to international competition, the need to curtail medical spending will intensify.

If health expenditures are to be effectively controlled, more consistent national policies will be required. Today, health policy in the United States is a curious blend of direct and indirect regulation, and price and nonprice competition. Cost controls and incentives for efficiency are unevenly applied across treatment settings and the rules and regulations of reimbursement vary from payer to payer. In this climate, the savings achieved by one payer or in one treatment setting are not net savings because they are offset by higher charges to other payers or expenditures in other treatment settings. The result is a non-system that is heterogeneous and uncoordinated almost to the point of chaos.

Should the nation reach a consensus that the amount of resources devoted to health care must be limited, it will face two general options for cost containment. The experience of other Western nations suggests that health care costs can be controlled through global budgeting. This usually takes the form of national health insurance (NHI), although some nations, like the United Kingdom, employ a national health service (NHS) where hospitals are owned and physicians are employed or contracted by the national government. Experience in these countries suggests that when health care spending is brought under the control of the national (or, as in Canada, national and provincial) government and forced to compete with other programs for tax dollars, expenditure growth is restrained (IECD, 1987).

More limited experience with competing HMO's suggests that price competition between vertically integrated health care delivery systems may restrain costs by substituting ambulatory and preventive services for inpatient hospital care (Manning et al., 1984). It is doubtful that current trends in the markets for private health insurance and medical services will bring about the development of integrated corporate systems on a scale necessary to achieve the required level of price competition without supportive government policies. In the absence of regulation, much of the competition will be diverted into nonprice avenues such as product differentiation, advertising, and the creation of unnecessary demand. In addition, it is doubtful that competition among individual physicians and hospitals will significantly curtail spending unless the market is dominated by efficient vertically integrated systems.

SUMMARY

The health service industry is undergoing rapid restructuring as government and private employers seek to contain health care spending. The change process is likely to continue for some time because no single clear policy direction has emerged. Today, the third-party reimbursement system sends mixed signals to providers as public and private payers seek to substitute incentives to conserve resources and treat patients in the least costly setting for incentives to overtreat and overuse inpatient hospital care. These reforms are occurring haphazardly as different payers incorporate different changes at different times. To date most reimbursement reforms have been applied to hospitals while physicians and patients face incentives to overtreat and overutilize. The result has been limited control of inpatient hospital costs largely offset by higher ambulatory spending.

Pressures for effective cost containment will increase as a result of the needs to reduce the federal budget deficit and enhance economic competitiveness. The experience of other Western industrialized nations suggests that global budgeting can restrain the growth of health care spending. More limited experience with HMO's suggests that competition between vertically integrated systems which combine the financing and delivery of medical services can restrain health cost inflation. Currently the most pressing need for the health care industry is a consensus regarding what shape the twenty-first century health care system should take and consistent policies to guide its evolution.

REFERENCES

Arnett, R. and G. Trapnell (1984). "Private Insurances: New Measures of a Complex and Changing Industry," *Health Care Financing Review* 6, 31-42.

Bailey, R. (1977). "An Economist's View of the Health Services Industry," in Louis Weeks and Howard Berman (eds.), *Economics in Health Care.* Germantown, MD: Aspen Systems Corp.

Califano, J. (1986). "A Corporate Rx for American Medicine: Managing Runaway Health Costs," *Issues in Science and Technology* 2, 81-90.

Caper, P. and M. Zubkoff (1984). "Managing Medical Costs Through Small Area Analysis," *Business and Health* 1, 20-25.

Coelen, C., and D. Sullivan (1981). "An Analysis of the Effects of Prospective Reimbursement Programs on Hospital Expenditures," *Health Care Financing Review* 2, 1-40.

Cromwell et al. (1987). "Comparative Trends in Hospital Expenses, Finances, Utilization and Inputs, 1970-81," *Health Care Financing Review* 9, 51-70.

Dever, A. (1980). *Community Health Analysis*. Germantown, MD: Aspen Systems Corp.

Eastaugh, S. (1981). *Medical Economics and Health Finance*. Boston: Auburn House.

Enthoven, A. (1980). *Health Plan*. Reading, MA: Addison-Wesley.

Etheredge, L. (1986). "The World of Insurance: What Will the Future Bring?" *Business and Health* 3, 5-9.

Farber, H. (1987). "The Recent Decline in Unionization in the United States," *Science* 238, 915-920.

Feldstein, P. (1983). *Health Care Economics*. 2d ed. New York: John Wiley and Sons.

Fieldstein, M. (1977). *The Rapid Rise of Hospital Costs*. Washington, DC: U.S. Council on Wage and Price Stability.

Freund, D., and E. Neuschler (1986). "Overview of Medicaid Capitation and Case-Management Initiatives," *Health Care Financing Review*, Annual Supplement, pp. 21-30.

Fuchs, V. (1974). *Who Shall Live?* New York: Basic Books.

Management Initiatives," *Health Care Financing Review*, Annual Supplement, pp. 21-30.

Gibson, R., and C. Fisher (1978). "National Health Expenditures, Fiscal Year 1977," *Social Security Bulletin* 41, 38-45.

Ginzberg, P., and M. Ostow (1984). *The Coming Physician Surplus: In Search of a Public Policy*. Totowa, NJ: Rowman and Allanheld.

Gizenberg, P., and F. Sloan (1984). "Hospital Cost Shifting," *New England Journal of Medicine* 310, 893-898.

Greenspan, N., and R. Vogel (1980, Spring). "Taxation and Its Effect on Public and Private Health Insurance and the Demand for Medical Care," *Health Care Financing Review* 1, 39-46.

Health Care Financing Administration (1979). *Professional Standards Review Organization 1979 Program Evaluation*. Washington, DC: Health Care Financing Administration.

Higgins, C., and E. Meyers (1987). "Managed Care and Vertical Integration: Implications for the Hospital Industry," *Hospital and Health Service Administration* 32, 319-327.

Hyman, H. (1975). *Health Planning: A Systematic Approach*. Germantown, MD: Aspen Systems Corp.

Inglehart, J. (1984). "The Twin Cities' Medical Marketplace," *New England Journal of Medicine* 311, 343-348.

Interstudy (1985). *The HMO Industry Ten Year Report*. Minneapolis, MN: Interstudy.

Jencks, S., et al. (1984, November). "Evaluating and Improving the Measure of Hospital Case-Mix," *Health Care Financing Review*, Supplement, pp. 1-11.

Manning, W., et al. (1984). "A Controlled Trial of the Effects of a Prepaid Goup Practice on Use of Service," *New England Journal of Medicine* 310, 1505-1510.

Masso, A. (1985). "HMOs in Transition: What the Future Holds," *Business and Health* 2, 21-29.

Matarazzo, J., et al. (eds.) (1984). *Behavioral Health*. New York: John Wiley and Sons.

Mayer, T., and G. Mayer (1985). "HMOs: Origins and Development," *New England Journal of Medicine* 312, 590-594.

Mayer, T., and G. Mayer (1987). *Financing and Delivering Health Care*. Paris: Organization for Economic Cooperation and Development.

Omenn, G., and D. Conrad (1984). "Implications of DRG's for Clinicians," *New England Journal of Medicine* 311, 1314-1317.

Organization for Economic Cooperation and Development (1987). *Financing and Delivering Health Care.* Paris: OECD.

Paringler, L. (1979). *The Medicare Assignment Rates of Physicians: Their Responses to Changing Reimbursement Policy.* Washington, DC: Health Care Financing Administration.

Patricelli, R. (1986). "Musings of a Blind Man—Reflections on the Health Care Industry," *Health Affairs* 5, 128-134.

Powills, S. (1985). "Blue's Program Divides Hospitals," *Hospitals* 59, 20.

Reinhart, U. (1986). "Quality Care in Competitive Markets," *Business and Health* 3, 7-9.

Relman, A. (1985). "Cost Control, Doctor's Ethics and Patient Care," *Issues in Science and Technology* 1, 103-111.

Rice, T., et al. (1985). "The State of PPO's: Results from a National Survey," *Health Affairs* 4, 25-40.

Ripps, J., and H. Werronen (1986). "Insurer-Provider Networks: A Marketplace Response," *Business and Health* 3, 20-22.

Russell, L. (1979). *Technology in Hospitals: Medical Advances and Their Diffusion.* Washington, DC: Brookings Institution.

Salkever, D., and T. Bice (1979). *Hospital Certificate-of-Need Controls.* Washington, DC: American Enterprise Institute.

Schick, A. (1987). "Controlling the Uncontrollables: Budgeting for Health Care in an Age of Megadeficits," in Jack Meyer and Masion Lewin (eds.), *Charting the Future of Health Care.* Washington, DC: American Enterprise Institute.

Sloan, F. (1981). "Regulation and the Rising Cost of Hospital Care," *Review of Economic Statistics* 63, 479-487.

Sloan, F., and B. Steinwald (1978). "Effects of Regulation on Hospital Costs and Input Use." Paper presented at the Annual Meeting of the American Economic Association, Chicago, IL, August 29.

Smits, H., et al. (1984, November). "Variation in Resource Use Within Diagnostic Related Groups: The Severity Issue," *Health Care Financing Review* Supplement, pp. 71-78.

Starr, P. (1982). *The Social Transformation of American Medicine.* New York: Basic Books.

Stern, R., and A. Epstein (1985). "Institutional Responses to Prospective Payment Based on Diagnosis Related Groups," *New England Journal of Medicine* 312, 621-627.

Sullivan, S., and R. Gibson (1983). *Restructuring Medicaid: A Survey of State and Local Initiatives.* Washington, DC: American Enterprise Institute.

Taylor, H., and M. Kagay (1986). "The HMO Report Card," *Health Affairs* 5, 81-89.

U.S. Congressional Budget Office (1979). "Controlling Rising Hospital Costs." Washington, DC: Government Printing Office.

U.S. General Accounting Office (1980). "Report to the Congress: Rising Hospital Costs Can Be Restrained by Regulating Payments and Improving Management." Washington, DC: Government Printing Office.

Woodall, G., et al. (1987). "Characteristics of the Frequent Visitor to the Industrial Medical Department and Implication for Health Promotion," *Journal of Occupational Medicine* 29, 660-664.

9

Humana, Inc.—A Business Perspective on Health Care

GEORGE L. ATKINS

Medical indigency is a growing problem for the U.S. health care delivery system. The country's excellent reputation for medical care rests upon the fact that most of the nation's sick can be helped due to the availability of advanced medical technology and well-trained health care professionals. However, the delivery of high-quality medical care is costly. The question of who will bear the brunt of that cost for the sick of America who are either poor or without health care insurance is one that this country desperately needs to resolve.

One of the first hurdles associated with developing creative solutions for the treating of those who are medically indigent is finding out the number of individuals who are either indigent or uninsured. Current estimates of the size of the medically indigent population are not precise, but they do give useful information as to the magnitude of this societal problem.

During the mid-1980s, approximately 35 million Americans had neither public nor private health insurance coverage. This figure represents one-sixth of the nonelderly population (those under age sixty-five) and one-seventh of the overall population.[1] An additional 5 to 18 percent of the population is suspected as having inadequate health care insurance coverage.[2] When both of these information sources are combined, it is estimated that about 50 million Americans are at risk of medical indigency.[3]

Adding to the problem of indigent people is the fact that the number of people under the age of sixty-five who have no medical insurance increased by 33 percent between 1979 and 1982.[4] Until 1979, health insurance coverage had steadily risen, but the economic recession resulted in losses of jobs, which in turn meant a loss of insurance. Today, nearly 66 percent of those who are uninsured are working adults and their dependents.

Uncompensated care, or the total amount of unpaid charges attributable to charity and bad debt, increased by 50 percent in real terms, that is, a percentage adjusted for inflation, according to the American Hospital Association. In 1982 uncompensated care reached $6.2 billion.[5]

Over 50 percent of the uncompensated care provided in U.S. hospitals today results from accidents and maternity care cases. In addition, about 33 percent of those without medical insurance do not pay their hospital bills.[6] In 1983 a study by the American Hospital Association showed that uncompensated care accounted for 11.5 percent of public hospitals' charges. The same study pointed out that uncompensated care was 4.2 percent of not-for-profit hospitals' charges and 3.1 percent of for-profit hospitals' charges.[7]

A study in the early 1980s by the Robert Wood Johnson Foundation indicates that the growing number of uninsured and medically indigent are finding it hard to obtain necessary medical attention. The study reports that uninsured individuals were found to be three times more likely to be refused necessary medical attention for financial reasons. The report concludes that "more than 12 percent of Americans (28 million people) appear to have particularly serious trouble coping with the U.S. health care system and obtaining medical care when they need it."[8]

What reimbursement for indigent medical care there is, is largely financed through government appropriations. When no reimbursement exists for a hospital's delivery of indigent medical services or when there is only partial reimbursement, the unpaid portion is supplemented by a hospital's private paying patients through a process commonly called "cost shifting."

Cost shifting, which has long been a part of the U.S. health care delivery system, involves subsidizing indigent health care with private patients' costs at both public and private hospitals. In the system of cost shifting, employers and private insurers carry the weight by being charged higher hospital charges and by paying and charging higher health insurance premiums.

Until the early 1980s and the advent of the Prospective Payment System, employers and insurers supported the practice of cost shifting with little hesitation. But in today's cost-contained health care environment, the cost-shifting mechanism is breaking down. Today, employers prudently can purchase health care insurance coverage that costs the company and the employee less money but in turn, does not have the financial slack to cover the costs of indigent care. In addition, the federal government's attempts over the past several years to trim away the country's budget deficit have made the public sector unable to absorb the costs of indigent care.

Today's U.S. indigent health care picture looks like this: a large medically indigent population, a growing number of medically uninsured, and cost-conscious hospitals and insurance organizations that can no longer justify "free care" for either growing sector.

The Commonwealth of Kentucky, and particularly Jefferson County, where Louisville (population 679,300) is located, is not immune to the national crisis associated with medical indigency. The Kentucky state legislature and courts have ruled that the state's 120 counties have statutory responsibility for funding medical treatment for indigents. In reality economic support for indigent health care has been shared among all levels of government and the private sector.

In Jefferson County itself an estimated 71,000 residents, including over 25,000 children, are at risk of medical indigency.[9] The Kentucky Medical Assistance Program, the state's Medicaid program, is the largest source of medical indigency funding. However, because of the state's weak tax base and low eligibility standards for KMAP coverage, the program is unable to support the 15 percent of the state's population, or about 400,000 residents, who fall below the federal poverty line. Eligibility requirements show that a family of four must have a net adjusted income of less than $3,900 to qualify for the Kentucky Medical Assistance Program.

Indigent patients in the Louisville area and the rural areas surrounding Louisville have historically received medical care at the public hospital located in Louisville. The city used state funds to build the first public hospital in the early 1800s to care for the mariners who became sick while traveling the Ohio River. Over the next hundred years, the hospital expanded its services to the poor with money from the city's treasury. Also during that time, the hospital became affiliated with the University of Louisville School of Medicine.

In 1914, a new city hospital, later called General Hospital, was built. For the next seventy years, this facility, which came to be known as "Old General," was the primary public hospital in Louisville and the area's major medical teaching hospital. By the early 1970s, it was quite clear that a new public hospital was needed because "Old General's" overcrowded space and forty-bed wards were hampering the delivery of quality care and were threatening the future accreditation of the University of Louisville's School of Medicine (see Illus. 9.1).

In 1976, construction, financed primarily by the state government, began on a new $73 million complex. The complex consists of a 404-bed hospital and outpatient services and support services building (Illus. 9.2). General Hospital changed its name to University Hospital and was deeded to the University of Louisville. But by 1982, as the new facility was near completion, the hospital's opening was threatened by four factors plaguing the University of Louisville:

- During the 1970s, three separate management groups had tried unsuccessfully to maintain the hospital's financial viability while underwriting huge uncompensated care costs.

- The cost of treating indigent patients had grown 20 percent faster than the government funds to pay for it.

- The old hospital faced potential operating deficits of up to $5 million per year, and at that time, some indigent patients were being turned away.

- The city and county governments said they could not increase their funding for indigent care at the same time that outside consultants were telling the university that the new hospital complex would be even more expensive to operate.

By 1982 Louisville's only public hospital was in desperate need of financial

Illus. 9.1 A typical ward in the old University Hospital.

Illus. 9.2 Humana Hospital–University consists of three buildings: the concentrated care building (center of photo), the ambulatory care building, and the institutional services center and parking garage. (Humana Hospital–University)

help, and the university put out a plea for assistance. The first suitor offering to run the hospital was NKC Inc., a not-for-profit corporation in Louisville that operates two of the city's hospitals. However, NKC's offer was to take over the hospital but not take on the hospital's financial risk. In its proposal, NKC offered to guarantee access for the medically indigent up to the level of government funding and offered to pay the government $1.00 per year for rent.

David A. Jones, long-time Louisville resident and chief executive officer and chairman of the board of Humana, Inc., with corporate headquarters in Louisville, was concerned when he heard of NKC's offer. He decided that Humana could do better. Humana is an investor-owned health care corporation that owns and manages eighty-five hospitals in the United States and abroad and offers a family of flexible health benefit plans.

In July 1982 Humana announced its proposal. It offered to lease the hospital at its market value and to assume full financial risk for the care of the medically indigent, on the condition that the city, county, and state governments would maintain their existing levels of funding to the hospital. Humana made such a bold offer because it was sure that the hospital facility could attract private patients as well as indigent ones.

The Commonwealth of Kentucky, Louisville, Jefferson County, the University of Louisville, and Humana finalized their unique partnership agreement in January 1983. The Humana Hospital–University agreement is comprised of three separate contracts, including a lease agreement with the state, an affiliation agreement with the University, and a quality and charity trust fund agreement with all the governmental entities.

Under the lease agreement between Humana and Kentucky, Humana paid the state $6.5 million annually for the first four years and $6 million annually thereafter for the hospital facility. The lease is renewable for nine four-year terms. Humana assumes responsibility for the hospital's management and is entitled to run it as a for-profit facility. Humana also assumes responsibility for repairs, maintenance, capital improvements, and insurance for the facility.

Under the affiliation agreement between Humana and the University of Louisville, Humana agreed to provide the following funds to the university:

- 20 percent of the hospital's annual pretax profits
- $4 million to support medical services and education programs at the hospital, paid during the fifth year of the partnership
- Interest on the $4 million during each of the first four years to support these services
- A percentage of the costs of salary plus all benefits for 174 medical residents the first year and a negotiated number thereafter
- Salary for administrative heads of the medical and dental schools for their work as chiefs of services for the hospital

In addition, the affiliation agreement calls for membership on the hospital board to include four university representatives and encouragement from the university for admission of patients from private practices to the hospital.

Under the trust fund agreement, Humana promised to provide necessary inpatient care for all indigents in Jefferson County and to admit all emergency patients regardless of residence or ability to pay. In return, the three governments agreed to provide Humana $19.8 million for the first full year and agreed that the fund would be increased each year thereafter by the lesser of either the percentage increase of the respective governments' tax revenue or the consumer price index.

The Quality and Charity Care Trust Agreement also includes several other stipulations. Ninety percent of this fund is to be used to provide medically necessary indigent care for Jefferson County. At the point that government funds are depleted, Humana assumes the risk to provide care at its own expense. Up to 10 percent of the fund is being used to provide medically necessary inpatient care for adult indigents living outside Jefferson County. While there is no contractual obligation to provide care over the 10 percent fund amount, all those living outside Jefferson County and needing care have been admitted. An independent ombudsman resolves any disagreement over indigent patient eligibility and has the authority to require the hospital to admit a patient.

During the first four years of the partnership agreement, the city, county, and state have put $89,444,000 in the Quality and Charity Trust Fund. During that time, services for the medically indigent have amounted to $127,366,000, and Humana absorbed $37,922,000 of that in unreimbursed care.

Inherent to developing the Charity Care and Trust Agreement was developing a definition of "indigent." For the purpose of the fund, an indigent person is defined as:

1. Not eligible for any government health insurance program, not covered by a private insurance plan, or one whose coverage for hospital care from private insurance, Medicare or Medicaid is depleted.

2. Having income from all sources equal to or less than that required to qualify for free or reduced cost care under the federal Hill-Burton Program, using income poverty guidelines to the Louisville area. For example, a family of four living in the Louisville area would have to have a combined annual income of $11,060 or less to qualify.

The agreement between Humana, the university, and the three governments addresses three questions, specific to Louisville, but applicable to any region of the nation. First, who will provide indigent hospital care in Louisville and Jefferson County? How will indigent care in this area be financed? How can quality and financial stability be built into a medical education and research program at a large, urban teaching hospital?

Each of the agreement's participants brought reservations to the table when the partnership was being formulated. Nowhere in the country had an agreement such as this ever been attempted. There was no business model to follow because Humana Hospital–University would become the first major public hospital to be operated by an investor-owned health care corporation.

The University of Louisville had several specific problems that it was eager to solve. First, it had no start-up capital to open the new hospital facility, to purchase new medical equipment for the facility, or to use to cover operating expenditures. The University of Louisville had no expertise in hospital management, and its personnel were not trained in the details of today's cost-contained health care environment. In addition, because of the bad conditions at the old hospital facility, the hospital's accreditation of its teaching programs was beginning to be problematic.

But even with all the university's needs, the hospital's faculty and administration hesitated before committing to the Humana offer because they were afraid that the teaching facility's staff would lose its academic freedom within the public/private joint venture.

All three government entities (state, county, and local) were in a position of either finding the funds to open the new hospital facility or at least sharing this economic responsibility with the university. The local government of Jefferson County was also concerned about how indigent medical care would be provided in the region if the new hospital was made nonpublic.

Humana, through the eyes of David Jones, saw a responsibility for helping the area's indigent by keeping the public hospital open and well managed. Even though Humana was aware of its long-standing reputation for efficiently operating community hospitals, the corporation was hesitant because it had never operated a teaching hospital and because there were no upper limits on the financial responsibility that Humana was assuming.

But there was a community need—the very great need of providing indigent health care. Humana felt that with the promise of a stable source of reimbursement, be it government funds or Medicaid reimbursement, the health care corporation had the management resources to be able to step in and take a chance on successfully running the teaching hospital.

After the agreement's fourth year of operation in 1987, Humana reassessed its commitment to the hospital and to the public. Undoubtedly, the private/public relationship has paid off for the governments, the university, the hospital, and for Humana, so much that David Jones recently announced Humana's intention to extend the agreement to a minimum of twelve years, or through 1995.

When Humana announced it was extending the agreement, University of Lousiville president Donald C. Swain said, "This agreement is a model for inpatient indigent care due to Humana's boldness and willingness to undertake risks. This very innovative and bold move solved a lot of problems for the University of Louisville."

In essence, University Hospital's reputation of the "Hospital of Last Resort" has been changed to the "Hospital of Choice" under Humana's management. This has been achieved, in large part, through bringing in new fields of high technology and offering specialized medical programs and services.

During the first four years of the agreement, Humana Hospital–University has expanded and improved its trauma services, allowing it to be ranked among the top trauma centers in the United States. It is the only institution in the state to be designated a Level 1 Trauma Center by the American College of Surgeons. The trauma center is connected with X-ray facilities and with the adult burn unit. The center is also supported by the STAT Flight Air Ambulance Service, which has transported over 2,000 trauma patients to the hospital over the past four years.

Humana Hospital–University has become the second largest provider of obstetrical service in the state, having delivered over 9,000 newborns during the past four years (Illus. 9.3). Also gaining attention is the University of Louisville Heart Save Program, which offers urgent twenty-four hour treatment of heart attack victims by an in-house cardiologist.

The hospital's Center for Applied Microcirculatory Research, established in 1986 with a $1.4 million grant from Humana, is investigating methods of applying microcirculatory science to important areas of clinical medicine. Another new program applies laser technology and drug therapy to the treatment and removal of certain types of cancerous tumors in the esophagus, lungs, colon, bladder, and rectum.

The implantation of multichannel cochlear implants, which are designed to restore partial hearing to the profoundly deaf, is another highly specialized service offered by the hospital. As one of very few U.S. institutions that has federal approval to implant the Kolff cochlear implant, Humana Hospital–University recently has been instrumental in conducting research and developing surgical techniques to perfect this procedure.

The acquisition of one of the community's few magnetic resonance imaging units in 1986 greatly increased the hospital's capability to deliver specialized care. The $3.1 million unit is a noninvasive diagnostic tool for diseases of the brain and spine.

The hospital's five-bed adult burn care unit provides the community's only specialized service for adult burn victims (Illus. 9.4). This unit was not scheduled to be in service during the first year of the partnership agreement, but because of the acute need for a place to care for burn victims, the opening was moved forward to January 1984. Since then, the unit has cared for 300 patients.

In addition to being able to expand its services under Humana's cost-effective system of management, Humana Hospital–University has been able to elevate the quality of patient care. The first change made by Humana's management team was to open the lines of communication between the hospital's administration, the university faculty, and the residents. With input from all these sources, Humana developed a strategic plan with a philosophical core of

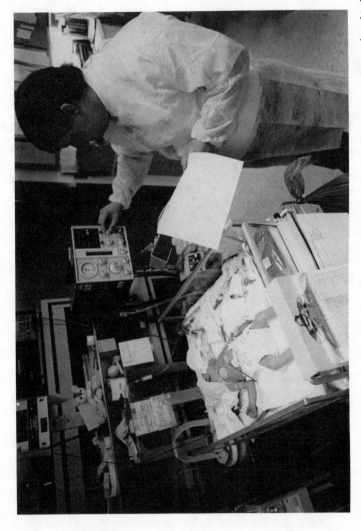

Illus. 9.3 The twenty-four-bed neonatal intensive care unit is one of the hospital's intensive maternal and infant health services that enable it to care for high-risk pregnancy patients and newborns with special needs. (Humana Hospital–University)

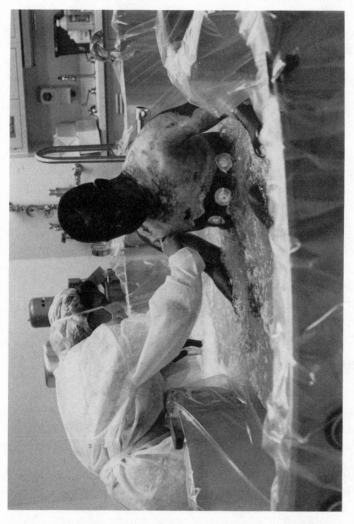

Illus. 9.4 The hospital five-bed adult burn unit provides the community's only specialized care for adult burn patients, who are highly susceptible to infection and require concentrated care and extensive treatment and therapy. (Humana Hospital–University)

"management by objective." Under the plan, each hospital department operates within a standardized system and is subject to quarterly review.

The management team also developed a hospital quality assurance program that is supervised by a committee made up of medical staff members, nursing administrators, and representatives from each medical service area. This committee monitors patient care services and recommends corrective action if an optimal level of quality is not being provided. The hospital's utilization review program assures that each patient admitted to the hospital receives timely and appropriate care and is treated in the most cost-effective manner possible.

Contributing to its operational success has been the hospital's ability to reap the economic benefits of being part of a corporation as large as Humana. Specifically it has been able to establish national purchasing contracts through the health care corporation. Pharmaceuticals, surgical supplies, major medical technology, disposables, laundry services, and food service all become significantly cheaper when they are purchased or negotiated in bulk, as Humana has been able to do with its hospitals worldwide. Because of its association with Humana, the hospital has also been able to take advantage of the corporation's computer capabilities and management information systems benefits.

Humana's management team has instituted reforms to control costs at the hospital as well as increase productivity at the facility. One of Humana's objectives in the agreement was to bring more privately insured patients to the public hospital, and it has succeeded. Prior to the agreement, the hospital averaged thirty-four privately insured patients per day, or less than 10 percent of the total census. During fiscal 1987, this number has risen to eighty-five or 21 percent of the total census. This increase is primarily attributable to Humana's increased technology and quality of service, but also to the willingness of the university faculty to admit their own private patients.

In addition, during a time of nationwide decreases in hospital occupancy, Humana Hospital–University's overall census has climbed from a 55 percent occupancy rate before the opening of the new hospital to 1987's 68 percent rate. Humana has also streamlined the number of employees at the hospital and improved operating procedures, with both changes resulting in a 17 percent decrease in operating expenditures since its opening.

According to Gary Sherlock, vice president of Humana's central region, "The essence of the arrangement is that one well-managed, conveniently located hospital with a base of existing business was able to add a large prepaid group with at least minimum financial coverage, thereby significantly lowering unit costs, which in turn enabled it to cap government's financial commitment while solving the community's vexing indigent care problem."[10]

The public and private sector agree that Humana has made significant achievements at Humana Hospital–University during its first four years of management from 1983 to 1987, especially in the teaching program where

Humana has contributed $27,612,000 to enhance research, faculty, and programs. Some noted achievements include:

1. Humana provided over $4.88 million from pretax profits to the University of Louisville for use in operating its medical school and for enhancing the teaching program. In addition to this sum, interest totaling $1.59 million from a $4 million grant was contributed by Humana to support the university's medical teaching programs.
2. Humana offered further support for the university's teaching mission by providing funding for 713 residencies. Currently, Humana is funding 184 resident physicians, or 40 percent of the medical school total, at an annual cost of $4 million.
3. Humana allocated over $16 million in capital expenditures for the acquisition of new equipment for the hospital and for improvements to the facility.
4. Humana absorbed $37.9 million out of operating revenues for indigent care rendered over and above government funding.
5. Humana contributed $2.3 million to support the hospital's outpatient clinics—financial support that was not required by the Partnership Agreement.
6. Humana paid over $2.8 million in income and sales tax revenues and $28 million in lease payments to the Commonwealth of Kentucky. Federal income taxes amounted to more than $7.6 million.
7. Humana provides employment for approximately 1,500 metro Louisville residents at the hospital.
8. Humana increased the number of medically indigent patients who were treated by 21.4 percent between January 1986 and January 1988.
9. Humana has also helped the local governments to decrease their spending for contributions to the hospital. For example, in 1978-1979, the city of Louisville contributed 4.3 percent of its total budget to the hospital, and Jefferson County contributed 6.2 percent. But in 1986-1987, the city's contribution had decreased to 2.0 percent.

As Robert H. Waterman, Jr., stated in his book on American business, *The Renewal Factor*: "There is no magic in the way Humana turned the place around. It was work, but they simply did the thing they do well. For Humana, the magic is in the adventure of taking a risk that nobody on the outside thinks is possible, turning it into a cause, making it work, and enabling the whole organization to feel proud of itself for doing so well."

An objective study of the "new" Humana Hospital–University was conducted in 1986 by Penn + Schoen Associates. The survey questioned twenty-six physicians at Humana Hospital–University and public officials and members of other interested parties. The purpose was to attempt to assess physicians' and public officials' attitudes toward the workings of the public/private partnership.

According to the study, both area physicians and public officials agreed that Humana Hospital–University is doing a very effective job in providing health care to indigents. Of the doctors at Humana Hospital–University 91 percent said that overall operations have improved. About 90 percent of Humana Hospital–University physicians said that the volume of patients has increased in their respective divisions, and 64 percent of the hospital's physicians said that indigents are better cared for than they were at the old University Hospital. One physician surveyed said, "Humana is much better at administration. . . . I have complete access to Humana management for my concerns."

In addressing overall objectives that the Partnership Agreement has not met, it is important to note that Humana has honored each of the contract stipulations. The intention of the agreement was not to address outpatient indigent care in Louisville. However, there are federal government funds that are currently available to one clinic and two family health care centers in Louisville. The grants and funding keeping these outpatient sites open have been significantly expanded since the Partnership Agreement set a precedent for inpatient acute care for medical indigents in Lousiville. Humana has always offered to provide inpatient acute care for medically indigent pediatric patients, but there is another medical facility in Louisville that is devoted to delivering care to this population segment.

Recently, the issue of the homeless in Louisville has become important. In response to the problem, a center near Humana Hospital–University recently applied for federal grants and received funding to aid the community's homeless. Even though this funding was totally separate from the Partnership Agreement, Humana suspects that the funding of this kind of program is being granted more readily because the government is aware of the unique effort in place to provide inpatient hospital care for the indigent.

One sometimes problematic issue inherent to the agreement that Humana still needs to work out is caring for out-of-state patients. While 100 percent of the funding comes from Kentucky government sources, the hospital has not yet denied care to any out-of-state medically indigent patients.

The current Partnership Agreement is a national model in that it was the first such arrangement in the United States and has become the basis of negotiations for others seeking similar arrangements. Academicians, politicians, hospital administrators, and news media from all over the nation, as well as Europe, Asia, and South America, have made site visits to investigate the advantages and disadvantages of the model. The apparent advantages include a stable source of funding for indigent care, capped government payments, guaranteed health care services for a defined population, improved operations and decreased costs, highest quality services and technology, the provision of capital for expansion, innovative programs and advanced medical technology, and additional resources for educational programs.

The disadvantages of the model are not so apparent. Often, those reviewing this public/private partnership have expectations that this "model" should solve all the medical indigency problems inherent to our country's health care delivery system. This expectation is beyond the scope of the project and was never an intended outcome.

Public/private partnerships may become more predominant in health care as hospitals' operating capital continues to erode, especially in public and teaching hospitals. Several environmental factors will also force changes in the way that future health care services will be delivered. These factors include:

- Industry segments will refuse to pay for costs not associated with the delivery of care to their specific patient populations, which will cause the industry to shift to alternate delivery and financing mechanisms further.
- Governments will decrease allocations that provide funds to the Medicare and Medicaid programs, indigent care, and education.
- World economic markets will continue to be in flux, causing further federal and state deficits.
- Decreased utilization of capital-intensive acute care and tertiary care facilities will lead to increases in costs at those facilities.
- Increased numbers of deductible insurance plans will be in force.
- Hospitals will have lower margins and more of them will verge on bankruptcy.

Today, hospitals' underlying motivation for seeking investor-owned business partners is capital. After the introduction of the Prospective Payment System, this country saw its first acquisitions of teaching hospitals by investor-owned health care companies. The reason is obvious. A teaching hospital's mission has always revolved around access to new medical technology and a diversified patient population, which includes those who are medically indigent. Teaching hospitals generally have not had the interest or motivation to concern themselves with financial worries. This is no longer the case.

Critics of public/private partnerships in health care, and specifically investor-owned management of teaching hospitals, consistently point to the allegation that under this type of management, tertiary hospitals are likely to discriminate against nonpaying patients, to have access only to medical technology that can generate a profit, and to be discouraged from costly educational and research practices. However, in the public/private health care arrangements that exist today, these fears are not being realized. As various surveys of existing arrangements point out, investor-owned health care companies are not purchasing teaching hospitals to disregard the institutions' commitment to education, research, and diversified patient populations, but to benefit from the reputation that these practices generate.

Investor-owned health care chains are unique partners for teaching hospitals. These corporations have the financial capacity to underwrite large capital expenditures required to purchase the latest medical equipment or start an innovative medical program. The larger corporations also have the ability to undertake the associated financial risk of managing a teaching hospital, including the hospital's diversified patient population's insurance status.

However, Humana does not say that the Parternship Agreement at Humana Hospital–University is a model that will solve the problem of indigent medical care in all situations. Certain "ingredients" must be necessary for a similar public/private partnership to be successful. These include:

1. A real need that is recognized by all parties involved.
2. The ability for the corporation to run the hospital as a well-managed facility without academic turf fights or government patronage.
3. A strong commitment by the government, university, and private sector to make the agreement work.

Also inherent to the success of this venture is the fact that all parties agreed that the entire thrust behind the Partnership Agreement is that indigent care is a societal issue. But for the first time in the health care industry, an investor-owned health care company decided to do something about indigent care instead of just debating about it. In a nutshell, indigent care was treated like any other hospital service. Humana offered the lowest bid to provide the service and was awarded the contract.

Another area in the public health care sector where similar action could be taken is the federal government's Medicaid program. Quite feasibly, the treatment of Medicaid patients, who are federally funded, could be limited to providers that the government is financially assisting because they have bid for this service, ensuring high quality at the lowest cost.

Privatization in health care probably even has a place outside exclusive agreements between a hospital and an investor-owned company. For instance, emergency medical services or ambulances, have traditionally been made available to a community through the city or county governments. Already a trend is emerging whereby city and county governments are asking for bids from privately owned companies who own and manage these ambulance services. The reason is clear. These companies, not the city or county governments, are the experts in running this type of business. So a community service, which in most cases was a drain on local treasuries, can become profitable under the right management, leaving precious tax dollars to go for some other community need.

Health care is a service industry. Even though its "service" is more precious and vital than that provided by other industries, there is no reason why it cannot be privatized. Humana's message, from experience, is this: anywhere in health care where quality of care can be maintained or even bettered, but at a lower cost, there is a distinct avenue for privatization.

NOTES

1. Margaret Sulvetta and Katherine Swartz, *The Uninsured and Uncompensated Care: A Chartbook*, National Health Policy Forum (Washington, DC, 1986), p. 101.

2. Pamela Farley, "Who Are the Uninsured?" *Milbank Memorial Fund Quarterly* 63, no. 3 (1985): 493.

3. American Hospital Association, Special Committee on Care for the Indigent, *Cost and Compassion: Recommendations for Avoiding a Crisis in Care for the Medically Indigent* (Chicago, 1986), p. 103.

4. U.S. Congress, Senate, Committee on Finance, Subcommittee on Health, *Hearing: Health Care for the Economically Disadvantaged*—Part I, 98th Congress, 2nd Session, p. 7.

5. American Hospital Association Council on Research and Development, *Health Care for the Indigent: Literature Review and Research Agenda for the Future* (Fall 1985), p. 10.

6. Frank Sloan, James Blumstein, and James Perrin, eds., *Uncompensated Hospital Care: Rights and Responsibilities* (Baltimore, 1986), pp. 19, 30, 189.

7. Institute of Medicine, *For-Profit Enterprise in Health Care* (Washington, DC, 1986), p. 102.

8. Robert Wood Johnson Foundation, *Updated Report on Access to Health Care for the American People* (1983), pp. 6-8.

9. "Report of the Task Force on Outpatient Indigent Care," Office of the Jefferson County Judge, July 15, 1986, pp. 6, 15.

10. Gary Sherlock, "Humana Turns University Hospital into a Success Story, Increase Care for Indigent," *Federation of American Hospitals Review*, March/April 1985, p. 63.

PART THREE

CONSTRAINTS AND OPPORTUNITIES

10

Legal Considerations in Privatization and the Role of Legal Counsel

MARK H. FLENER

As local, state, and federal governments are increasingly blurring the distinctions between government services and private industry, the legal ramifications of such activity must be explored. Government units are increasingly turning over their traditional public services to private companies. At the same time, they are using their favored legal status to grant incentives to private industry to locate within their boundaries. In the privatization of government services and the granting of incentives to private industry, a government unit must consider everything from labor to antitrust, securities, tax, and tort law.

While the previous chapters of this book have concentrated on the privatization of specific government services and alternative delivery systems, this chapter will explore some of the legal considerations that a government unit may encounter. In addition, it will outline the role that legal counsel plays in the granting of private contracts and incentives by a government unit. While an in-depth analysis of all the legal forces at work in privatization is not possible within the constraints of this chapter, it may be used by government officials as well as attorneys that counsel government units as a primer in the privatization legal process.

PROCEDURAL, TORT, AND CONTRACT CONSIDERATIONS

One form of privatization involves a government unit contracting with a private company for the performance of a traditional government service. By contracting out government services, the government unit enters into a contract directly with a private company. The terms of the contract are negotiated between the government unit and the private company as any legally binding obligation would be. In most contracting situations, the government unit will pay the private company directly for the services performed out of its tax revenues. For instance, a small town may hire out its garbage collection by contracting with a private company by paying an annual fee of $500,000, payable in monthly installments. This method allows the government unit control over the purse strings to ensure compliance by the private company.

The other popular method employed by government units seeking privatization of government services is the granting of a franchise. A franchise is a grant by a government unit to a private company of permission to furnish a service to the citizens of the government unit. Generally, the private company will perform the service and bill the citizens of the government unit directly. For example, in a franchise for garbage collection, the town would grant the private garbage company the exclusive right to collect garbage within the boundary of the government unit, and the private garbage company would then bill each citizen directly. This method allows the government unit to maintain some control over the garbage collection but not be involved in financing the service. It can also be seen as an indirect tax on the citizens for providing a government service.

Procedural Considerations

Once it has been decided that a government service should be carried out by a private company, the government's legal counsel plays an important role. The first concern of counsel must be fulfilling the procedural requirements of granting the contract or franchise.

Most state constitutions and statutes provide procedures for the bidding of contracts and franchises, the adoption of contracts by government units, and the granting of franchises by those government units. A government unit should ensure its compliance with all state constitutional and statutory requirements. If the contract or franchise is not properly adopted, the government unit may face challenges from losers in the bidding process who will seek to have the contract or franchise voided, or even seek damages from the government unit.

Not only could the loser of a government unit's bidding process challenge the contract, but the winner could as well. Suppose that a private company was awarded a five-year contract for the collection of garbage. After two years, the private company realized that its bid was too low, and it wanted out of the contract. If the contract was not properly bid or approved as required by law, the "winner" could seek to rescind the contract.

While each local and state government, as well as the federal government, has different procedural requirements, it is well for the government unit and legal counsel to consider the following:

• In initiating a contract proposal, make sure the advertising of the proposal and requests for bids are conducted according to local, state, and/or federal requirements;

• Insure that the application process allows sufficient time for competitive bidding;

• Insure that the government unit's contract and/or franchise is sufficiently informative, not vague; and

• Once a private company is selected, insure that the contract is properly approved by the governing body of the political unit.

Once the government unit has complied with all federal, state, and local procedural requirements, the private company can begin performance under the contract or franchise.

Tort Liability

Upon assumption by a private company of government services, another concern may face the government unit—that of tort liability for action or inaction of the private company. In considering the tort liability of a government unit, a brief discussion of sovereign immunity is in order.

Amendment XI of the United States Constitution denies persons access to the Federal courts in actions against the state. In addition, many state constitutions provide similar immunity to state and local government units. Yet today, courts and many state legislatures are increasingly chipping away at the doctrine of sovereign immunity. The emergence of insurance as well as a feeling that a local government unit should be held responsible for its actions have punctured the doctrine of sovereign immunity. Many state statutes provide that government units are immune from actionable wrongs if they maintain insurance coverage. Courts have also distinguished between the types of government units to determine immunity. Injured persons can also avoid problems of sovereign immunity by pursuing their claim under the Civil Rights Act by showing a deprivation of an individual's "rights, privileges, or immunities under color of any statute, ordinance, regulation, custom, or usage" (Civil Rights Act). In addition, an injured party may seek to bypass any immunity problem by bringing an action directly against the government unit's elected officials. While the details of sovereign immunity are beyond the scope of this chapter, it should be considered by counsel as the first line of defense to any tort claim brought against a government unit.

Assuming that the government unit is subject to an action, what standard will be applied to a city that has contracted away a traditional public service to a private company? With the recent advent of privatization as well as the use of alternative delivery systems, this question will be faced increasingly by the courts. In general, the courts have treated the liability of a government unit based on accepted principles of negligence. For an action of negligence to be maintained, there must be a duty, breach of that duty, and damages that were proximately caused by the breach of the duty (Posser, 1971).

The question then becomes: What duty does a government unit owe when it grants a private contract for the performance of a public service? In general, a government unit has a duty to comply with all procedural requirements as outlined previously. In addition, and more important in terms of tort liability, a government unit has a duty to investigate and examine the qualifications of the private company with whom it seeks to do business. This duty to examine and investigate can best be illustrated by an example.

Example 1. New Town wanted to enter into a private contract for the hauling and disposal of hazardous chemicals from New Town's water treatment plant. Illegal Dumping, Inc., made an offer to dispose of the hazardous chemicals that was more than 50 percent below the next competitive bid. New Town, without investigation into Illegal Dumping, Inc., let the contract to Illegal Dumping, Inc. A year later, residents of nearby Old Town experienced symptoms of nausea, weight loss, and an abnormal rate of miscarriages. After investigation, it was found that Illegal Dumping, Inc., has been improperly dumping the hazardous chemicals from New Town in Old Town's landfill. If the residents of Old Town can show that New Town did not thoroughly investigate Illegal Dumping, Inc., they could bring an action against New Town for the damages they have sustained. If a reasonable investigation would have shown that Illegal Dumping, Inc., was not reliable, residents of Old Town would succeed in their action against New Town.

It must be remembered, however, that a government unit is not a guarantor that the private company shall perform its obligations under the contract in a proper, nonnegligent manner. The government unit's duty is merely to investigate and assure itself of the legitimacy and ability of the private company to perform the contracted service. If New Town had thoroughly investigated Illegal Dumping, Inc., and found it a reliable company, New Town could not be liable for Illegal Dumping's negligence.

FINANCIAL INABILITY OF THE PRIVATE CONTRACTOR

One of the primary concerns of any government unit that is considering the privatization of a government service is ensuring delivery of the service by the private company. It is therefore imperative that the financial soundness of a company be established early in the bidding process. Legal counsel would be well advised to spell out the financial requirements of the government unit before a contract or franchise will be entered into. The government unit may satisfy itself by bonding requirements, review of financial statements and balance sheets, and requiring personal guarantees. Yet, no matter how careful a government unit is in selecting a financially sound private company, there may come a day when the private contractor is unable or unwilling to perform according to the terms of the contract.

At the early stages of a private company's difficulties, the private contractor may seek a slight increase in payments from the government unit (or, in a franchise, from the citizens of the government unit). The government unit may be faced with the difficult decision of refusing the increase or seeing the private company cease services to the residents of the government unit. Neither course is one that a government unit should take lightly. In deciding whether to allow a change in contract, the government unit should consider the following, upon advice from counsel:

- Likelihood that the private company will cease operations;
- Financial solvency of the company, either to obtain damages in the event of breach or to force specific performance of the contract;
- Cost of obtaining services from an alternative source;
- Legal and court costs of pursuing the private company;
- Impact on the residents of loss of services, even if only temporary;
- Reason for the financial difficulty, that is, did the company merely underbid in order to obtain the contract, or is the difficulty due to unforeseen costs?

When a government unit is unable or unwilling to grant the modification of contract or franchise, or where the private company can no longer provide the service regardless of assistance from the government unit, the government unit will be faced with a default by the private contractor. In such a case, the government unit will be forced to allow the private company out of the contract or franchise, or seek relief against the private company in the form of specific performance and/or damages.

In seeking specific performance, the government unit will force the private contractor to fulfill its duties under the contract. In the case of minor breaches in a contract, specific performance may be the government unit's simplest resolution. Yet, if the breach is material or the private company does not have the means (financial or otherwise) to carry out the terms of the contract, specific performance will not help.

Seeking damages may be the only option available to the government unit. In seeking damages for breach of contract between a government unit and private company, general contract law applies. The general rule in awarding damages for breach of contract is to award a sum that will put the nonbreaching party in as good a position as it would have been had the contract been performed (Dobbs, 1973). This can best be illustrated by an example.

Example 2. New Town had entered into a contract with Fly-by-Night Garbage Co. in which New Town paid Fly-by-Night $500,000 per year to pick up and dispose of the town's garbage. Fly-by-Night was unable to continue the contract when its chief executive officer stole $500,000 from the company's bank account. New Town obtained garbage collection immediately from Nationwide Garbage, Inc., for the sum of $750,000 per year. What damage claim would New Town have against Fly-by-Night? A claim for $250,000—the difference in the contract price of Fly-by-Night and Nationwide Garbage. This is known as the benefit of the bargain.

In addition to the benefit of the bargain, New Town may be entitled to consequential damages. Suppose that Fly-by-Night stopped garbage pick up, and that resulted in a major industry's decision not to locate in New Town. Could New Town recover damages as a result thereof? Again, general contract law applies. In order for consequential damages to be recoverable three requirements must be met:

1. New Town must prove that the consequential damages were in fact caused by the contract breach;
2. New Town must prove the amount of consequential damages with a reasonable degree of certainty; and
3. New Town must convince the court that the damages were within the contemplation of the parties at the time the contract was entered into (Dobbs, 1973).

If the company is solvent, the government unit should be able to recover damages upon a breach of contract. But if the private company is having financial difficulty, monetary damages may be unrecoverable.

A more troublesome problem develops for the government unit when the private contractor files for relief and protection under the United States Bankruptcy Code. A company that is having financial difficulty may elect to file for relief under either Chapter 7 or Chapter 11. The company can even wait until after a court judgment for damages has been rendered and then seek bankruptcy court protection.

Upon filing a petition for bankruptcy, the United States Bankruptcy Court enters an order of relief and automatic stay. In essence, this order prevents the government unit from taking any action against the private contractor in state court without obtaining permission of the bankruptcy court (by requesting relief of the automatic stay). If the company has filed a Chapter 7 Bankruptcy petition, the government unit's legal options are limited. A Chapter 7 filing means that the private company is to be liquidated and cease to exist. In the case of an individual, the Chapter 7 filing will, upon the granting of an order of discharge, relieve the individual of any legal liability toward the government unit.

In a Chapter 7 bankruptcy, the court or United States Trustee will appoint, or creditors elect, a trustee to sell unencumbered assets or assets with equity over and above any liens on the property. After deduction for costs of administration of the estate, the funds are paid on a pro rata basis to those creditors that have filed proper proofs of claims. While the majority of Chapter 7 bankruptcy cases have no funds to distribute, it would behoove a government unit's legal counsel to file its proof of claim in the event of a recovery.

While in a Chapter 7 bankruptcy proceeding the government unit has few options. It can generally proceed with granting a new contract for the private services formerly supplied by the now bankrupt company subject to the trustee assuming or rejecting any executory contract between the government unit and private company (discussed later).

In a Chapter 11 bankruptcy proceeding, the governmental unit will be faced with other options. A Chapter 11 bankruptcy is known as a reorganization bankruptcy. It has enjoyed increasingly favored status by financially troubled companies who seek to use the bankrupcty court to solve or ease their financial difficulties. Even very large companies such as Texaco have used Chapter 11 bankruptcy proceedings to their benefit. A Chapter 11 bankruptcy can be an effective tool for private companies to extract concessions from labor unions, creditors, and government units.

In a Chapter 11 bankruptcy, a financially troubled company seeks to restructure its debt through filing a plan of reorganization in bankruptcy court. The company in its plan can provide for a reduction or a complete elimination of unsecured debts and even a variation on the terms of its secured debts. The plan as proposed by the debtor is subject to a vote of creditors and in some cases may be forced on creditors by the court even without the necessary acceptance by creditors (called, appropriately, a "cramdown").

For a government unit that has used a private company for delivery of services, a Chapter 11 bankruptcy has an immediate impact. In a Chapter 11 proceeding, an automatic stay order is entered by the court. The government unit can take no action against the private contractor while this stay is in effect. In addition, a company in Chapter 11 is given 120 days to file a plan of reorganization, subject to extensions. The automatic stay provision of the bankruptcy code will hamper a government unit's ability to take action. In addition, an executory contract entered into between the government unit and the company can be accepted or rejected by the debtor company. Under the Bankruptcy Code, a contract that is ongoing and not fully performed is considered an executory contract (Collier, 1987). Most privatization contracts for the delivery of government services would fit into this category. If the contract is profitable for the debtor, it would be assumed that the company would accept the contract. If the contract is not profitable, it would be assumed that the debtor would reject it.

One trap government units and their legal counsel fall into when a Chapter 11 bankruptcy is filed is failure to take the initiative and force the debtor to take action. The Bankruptcy Code gives creditors (of which government units may be one) the right to force the company either to accept or reject the executory contract. The government unit can move the court early on to require the company to accept or reject the contract. If the company rejects the contract, the government unit can proceed with reletting bids and obtaining another company to carry out the services. If the company accepts the contract, the Bankruptcy Code requires the company to provide assurances that it can carry it out as well as provide a curing of the default. This is a potent weapon in the government's arsenal. The form of assurance will be left to the bankruptcy court but could take the form of bonding requirements, insurance coverage, personal guarantees, or other arrangements satisfactory to the court (Collier, 1987).

If the private contractor accepts the executory contract, cures the default, and provides adequate assurance of future performance, even a Chapter 11 proceeding will allow a continuation of service by the private contractor without major disruption. Again, an example of what can occur when a company seeks bankruptcy relief may be helpful.

Example 3. New Town and Fly-by-Night Garbage Company had entered into a contract whereby Fly-by-Night received $500,000 per year for garbage collection in New Town. After six months under the contract Fly-by-Night informed the city that they were having financial difficulty and sought a raise in the contract price. New Town refused, and Fly-by-Night Garbage Company filed for protection and relief under Chapter 11 of the Bankruptcy Code.

Upon Fly-by-Night's filing, the bankruptcy court entered an order staying all action against Fly-by-Night. This order prevented New Town from seeking damages or redress against Fly-by-Night. If garbage collection by Fly-by-Night is continuing, New Town may not be too concerned, but as soon as Fly-by-Night ceases garbage collection, New Town realizes some action must be taken.

Assuming that Fly-by-Night has ceased garbage collection, it is in default on its contract. New Town cannot, however, merely cancel the contract and find another garbage collector. New Town must first ask Fly-by-Night through the bankruptcy court to assume or reject the garbage contract. If Fly-by-Night rejects the contract, New Town is free to contract for another garbage collector. If Fly-by-Night accepts the contract, it must abide by its terms and collect garbage accordingly. Fly-by-Night cannot change the terms and conditions of the contract. In addition, Fly-by-Night must take corrective action to cure the default.

New Town may also be very skeptical of Fly-by-Night's acceptance of the contract. New Town can seek from Fly-by-Night "adequate assurance" of performance of the contract in the future by asking the bankruptcy court to require a personal guarantee from Fly-by-Night's owners, bonding, or a deposit into court of sufficient funds to guarantee performance.

PUBLIC FINANCING AND DEVELOPMENT OF PRIVATE COMPANIES

Government units are often called upon to finance a private industry either for the purpose of providing a government service or as incentives to a private company to locate within the boundary of the government unit. The governmental unit, in turn, would receive benefits from an increased tax base and growth. There are several methods used by government units to encourage and assist private companies. Among them are:

- innovation centers where the actual building to be used by private industries is constructed by the government unit;

- waiver of taxation by the government unit;
- site and road construction and preparation;
- providing of training for employees of the private industry by the government bonds.

In addition, one of the most often used methods is the issuance of government bonds. Bonds are a form of debt wherein the government unit promises to pay back a loan over a period of time at a specified or calculable rate of interest. Government units issue bonds not only to finance government projects but also for the benefit of private industry, known as private development or industrial bonds.

When a government unit decides to issue bonds for the financing of public or private development, it must insure compliance with all state and federal regulations. The Securities Act of 1933 and the Securities Act of 1934, while generally providing for the tax exemption of government-issued bond interest income, must still be carefully observed. The antifraud provisions of the Securities Act and court cases interpreting "due care" in the issuance of government securities must be reviewed and analyzed.

In the issuance of government bonds, like any other type of security, detailed legal analysis and opinions must be obtained. Indeed, before a bond issue can be sold to the general public, the government unit must provide a bond attorney's opinion letter. This opinion should be obtained from legal counsel knowledgeable in the laws and regulations involving the issuance of government bonds. The bond counsel will issue an opinion as to the status of the bonds and will set forth, among other things:

- the authority of the government unit to issue the bonds,
- the proper adoption of ordinance to sell bonds;
- whether there are liens upon property securing the bonds;
- and a certification as to the tax-exempt status under federal and state laws (Lamb and Rappaport, 1980).

As one can imagine, the opinion will be quite complex, expecially in regard to the tax treatment of the bond issue. Due to the technical nature of the opinion, as well as to the liability imposed by such an opinion, a government unit would be well advised to seek legal counsel experienced in such matters and not merely rely upon in-house counsel.

While the bond counsel issues an opinion as to certain factors, it must be remembered that the bond opinion does not go into the creditworthiness of the issuing government unit. If the government unit is suffering dire financial straits with the possibility of a default on their bonds that fact will not be part of the bond counsel's opinion letter. That fact, however, may very well have to be revealed as part of the bond issuance, or the government unit may face claims of fraud or lack of due diligence under various securities acts.

Bond Issuance under the Tax Reform Act of 1986

Before 1986, a government unit could issue bonds for public or private development without limit as long as the issuance of those bonds complied with state and federal guidelines. That has now changed significantly, with the result that government units are now limited in the amount of bonds they may issue for private development.

While an in-depth analysis of the changes brought about by the Tax Reform Act of 1986 is beyond the scope of this chapter, following is a brief account of major changes that should be reviewed by government units and their counsel at the early stages of bond issuance. The Tax Reform Act of 1986 changed the way government units could finance public and private projects by distinguishing between bonds for public services and those to aid private industry. Government-issued bonds' selling point is a result, in large part, of their tax-exempt status. Government units that issued bonds would have an advantage over the private sector in that the government bond issues were tax-exempt. Interest earned on government bonds by the investor was not taxed, thereby making them more attractive to the investor. Without this favored tax status, government units would have to compete with private bond issues at a comparatively high rate of interest.

The Tax Reform Act of 1986 now divides tax-exempt bonds into traditional government bonds and private activity bonds. For the most part, the financing of traditional government services is not as affected by the act's changes as is the ability of local governments to issue bonds to finance private industrial development, but amendments to the act have made government bonds somewhat less attractive.

The act now places a cap on the amount of private activity bonds that can be issued. Under the act, any issuance of bonds wherein 10 percent or more of the proceeds are to be used for private business is subject to the cap, as are industrial development bonds.

The act provides that the cap on issuance of government bonds shall be controlled at the state level. Each state (and local government units within that state) is allowed to issue no more than a specified dollar amount of bonds. The cap is calculated on the basis of per capita income of the residents of the state. This cap will prevent local government units from issuing bonds without approval of the appropriate state agency. In addition, local government units within a state may find themselves competing with each other for the privilege of issuing government bonds. Private industry may now look to those states that have not yet exhausted their cap on the issuance of private development bonds, and it may also require government units to be more selective in the issuance of private development bonds (Arey and O'Connor, 1987). Again, an example of how the cap on industrial development bonds might affect a government unit may be helpful.

Example 4. New Town, located in State Y, is interested in attracting a major manufacturing plant, Autoparts Manufacturing. New Town considers various methods to attract Autoparts, including the granting of property tax incentives, building of public access roads, and various other methods. Autoparts, however, is interested in having New Town finance the building of its plant by the issuance of industrial development bonds.

New Town consults the appropriate state agency and is told that the state and local government units have reached the cap placed on the issuance of industrial development bonds, and therefore the state cannot approve New Town's request. Autoparts decides to locate its plant in State X.

In order to prevent this from happening, New Town may be able to convince Autoparts to wait to build its plant until the next calendar year, when a new quota will be established for government units. In addition, New Town may take an aggressive stand by lobbying at the state level to prevent other local government units within State Y from receiving approval of their industrial development bonds.

CONCLUSION

In all aspects of our society, the law plays an ever-increasing role. In the relatively new area of privatization of government services, the law is in constant motion. The courts and legislative bodies have always given favored treatment to government units. Yet, with the merger of government units and private industry, the courts and legislative bodies are facing new challenges. The challenges of privatization have caused the courts and legislatures to take a careful look at the blurring distinction between private and public functions. The merger of government and private industry means that courts and legislatures will be called upon to rethink traditional legal reasoning as it has been applied to government units in the past.

The United States Congress has reacted, in part, to this trend by making it more difficult for government units to issue private development bonds (Tax Reform Act of 1986). Courts are increasingly holding government units responsible for actions of private companies when the distinctions of public and private are blurred. As a result of these changes, government officials, managers, and attorneys must keep abreast of the legal trends that may have an impact on privatization of government services.

REFERENCES

Arey, Patrick K., and O'Connor, Julie M. (1987). Tax-Exempt Obligations after the Tax Reform Act of 1986—A Brief Guide for the Local Government Attorney. *The Urban Lawyer*, 19, 1051-1065.

Bankruptcy Code, 12 U.S.C. Section 101 et seq. (1988).

Civil Rights Act, 42 U.S.C. Section 1983 (1979).

Collier, William Miller. (1987). *Collier on Bankruptcy* (Vols. 1-9). New York: Matthew Bender.

Dobbs, Dan B. (1973). *Handbook on the Law of Remedies*. St. Paul, MN: West.

Lamb, Robert, and Rappaport, Stephen P. (1980). *Municipal Bonds: The Comprehensive Review of Tax-Exempt Securities and Public Finance*. New York: McGraw-Hill.

Prosser, William L. (1971). *Handbook of the Law of Torts*. St. Paul, MN: West.

Securities Act of 1933, 15 U.S.C. Section 77a (1933).

Securities Act of 1934, 15 U.S.C. Section 77b (1934).

Tax Reform Act of 1986 (1987). *United States Code Annotated Special Pamphlet*. St. Paul, MN: West.

11

Introducing Entrepreneurial Competition into Public Service Delivery*

LAWRENCE K. FINLEY

The people in the best position to offer alternative production of services now being delivered by a city or other government are those who are familiar with the needs and are entrepreneurial in their businesses. Public services are ripe for innovative solutions to problems of cost and quality.

In business, familiarity borne of experience is often critical to cost and quality advantages. Studies have shown that 50 to 100 percent of new high-tech companies make products similar to those in which their founder had prior experience. In fact, prior experience with any particular product or service is probably the best predictor of an entrepreneur's success. Whether the entrepreneur ventures with partners to form a new company or joins an existing company to contract with a city, experience provides opportunity for a competitive advantage. There are no shortcuts to a thorough understanding of needs of public service production.

Much has been written in the past decade about privatization. More has been written than is known, since descriptive stories have been mixed with ideology and advocacy. I will suggest techniques—a process—that entrepreneurs will find helpful in competing with governments and other producers for work now performed by monopolistic governments. While government may legitimately be the sole provider for certain services (decide what, how much, to whom), the production (or delivery) of those services ought to be performed by the most able.

*Based on this author's "An Entrepreneurial Process for Privatization at the Local Level," *Privatization Review*, Winter 1987.

Before offering a process—action steps—a consideration of certain characteristics of public-private action will be helpful. To rush into a proposal or a bid for new business without a foundation of understanding of economic forces and parties involved would be needlessly risky and wasteful of time. A careful machine operator, upon shearing a drive pin, does not rush to replace the pin but rather investigates the forces on that pin, the hardness of the shaft, and the hardness of optional replacement pins.

ECONOMIC AND TECHNOLOGICAL FORCES

Economic forces that have an impact on the alternate delivery of services are primarily economies of scale and experience, competition, and technology. The nature of change in goals, toward efficiency and lower cost, or toward quality, should also be studied by the entrepreneur. The parties who influence choice of producer at the city level are the mayor and city council, city manager, department heads, other employees, clients (service users), active citizens, private competitors, and the media. Each merits special attention because each has its special interests and opportunity to move decisions toward those interests. In the language of business strategy the entrepreneur must understand cost structures, market forces, decision makers, and his own competitive strengths and weaknesses. The entrepreneurs who have competitive advantages will be able to sell the kinds of services they produce and then sell their specific companies as producers. *Experience effects* are perhaps the most important force for altering service production. Evidence suggests that for every doubling of experience at a task, costs can be cut between 10 and 20 percent (Abell, 1979). Scale and experience effects often overlap as they do in the following situations.

Experience effects that may open entrepreneurial opportunity in the public sector include compliance, pattern multiplying, and specialization. *Compliance* experience occurs when a company successfully complies with standards for water quality, effluent levels, air pollution, air traffic safety, diagnostic-related groups of illness treatment costs, or other performance areas. A city gains experience at bringing into compliance only one water treatment plant, for example. However, an entrepreneur in this business has opportunities for compliance at significant cost reductions when it transfers the experience from one city to a second, from these two to numbers three and four, and so on (Finley, 1984).

Pattern multiplying experience occurs when the design and construction of a facility for one client can be largely replicated for another. This experience occurs in design and construction of hospitals, nursing homes, water treatment plants, prisons, and other facilities. Pattern multiplying is a key to the efficiencies of chain stores and "package franchising" in the private sector. These potential experience savings are recently being appreciated by governments.

Specialization of labor allows efficiencies and effectiveness. A bill collection company can specialize in a government fee-for-service program. A sizable company may be built around trimming and removal of trees in several cities, while for individual cities there is not enough such work to allow extensive specialization of labor or equipment. Through specialization a company is expected to simplify subtasks and then employ lower-skill personel and higher-cost machines can be used. Cases of alternative service delivery suggest that this is happening.

Competition is the third major economic force supporting alternate delivery. We suggest that this is more accurately the fight for economic survival. When a competitor firm in a market loses enough bids or customers or loses a key contract, it goes out of business. Erroneously, it is often said that private ownership or operation per se leads to efficiency. There is no evidence for this ideological assertion. However, strong anecdotal evidence and certain rigorous studies show that competition does lead to extra efforts (Caves et al., 1981; Pescatrice and Trapani, 1980).

Competition merits further examination. Is all competition alike? Who benefits from competition? Is competition always preferred to no competition? Competition varies. In a children's recreational neighborhood soccer league where team standings are not officially recorded, most of the emphasis is on building bodies, motor skills, and social skills. Games (between competing teams) are provided as a means to these ends. By contrast, in nature, plants compete for water, nutrients, and sunlight with the result that the winners live and the losers die. Wild animals compete fiercely for food with like results. The children's sports competition has smaller cost (undesired effects), but business competition has costs of a kind unacceptable to many—dead jobs. Yet high stakes—big incomes for winners and lost jobs for losers—make competition a potent force for better public service. Third parties, those the competitors promise to serve, usually benefit.

The entrepreneur watching the privatization drama progress to the competition act is left cautious and ambivalent. While he may look longingly at the huge budgets of governments and wish for a share of that business, he prefers less competition, not more. Rationally he should want to substitute himself as monopolist for the city as monopolist.

Long-term contracts reduce competition but may benefit the public by inducing entrepreneurial investment, for example in airport facilities. Bid rigging reduces competition, obviously without commensurate benefits. Stories are prevalent of long-term contracts and even bid rigging whereby services are admittedly privatized, but competition is kept insignificant. Accounts of efficiency or effectiveness successes from competition travel the trade presses and word-of-mouth circuits so that public decision makers understand the importance of competition, not just privatization.

Technological innovation is the fourth force behind private services worth examination (Porter, 1980). Innovations in automated garbage handling, water treatment, sewage treatment, and other services can have far-reaching effects. Radically different processes of water treatment can make the experience of a city department obsolete. New computerized bookkeeping, billing, and database technologies can do the same to whole departments in bureaucratic governments.

Innovations in cable broadcasting, descramblers, and pay-TV all alter the nature of previously public goods. Broadcast programming has had the characteristics of a public good and is dominated by governmental production in most countries. These three innovations all shift programs away from the public good category by enabling exclusion of nonpayers.

In health care the invention of technically sophisticated, costly diagnostic and treatment equipment and processes pushes the industry toward privatization. Private financing is often more effective for these facilities and equipment (Touche Ross and Co., 1985). Private health care operations are replacing public in many markets. Portable treatments for kidney disease, cancer, and other illnesses push this treatment from the public hospital to the private home. Home health care by entrepeneurial companies is expected to double or triple in the next fifteen years.

In sum, the experienced entrepreneur and business have a number of potential forces on which to build services to cities. How do you sell these as advantages, beneficial to your targets, the public service decision makers? Who are these people? What are the probable goals and interests of each?

TWO GENERIC APPROACHES TO BUSINESS TARGETING

There are two generic approaches to targeting a city service to add to a business. Following the first approach, identify services that are contracted out in a large number of cities. Then identify cities, in locations where you could perform one of these services, that do not contract this service. The assumption is that a service that is widely contracted is tangible and readily monitored and thus a candidate for you to contract for. The International City Managers Association (ICMA) periodically surveys its members and then publishes responses showing which services are most commonly produced in-house, which are partially contracted out, and which are predominantly contracted. (A derivative of this approach is to identify services being unsatisfactorily produced, whether in-house or through contract. You then exploit that dissatisfaction by offering better quality or lower cost.)

The first approach requires the entrepreneur to transfer the organization's skills to the needs found. You may have to adapt a technology you possess to the requirements of a certain service. If you have data processing or MIS skill, it is readily transferable from a business to a public application, as are plumbing, maintenance, and others.

A second approach to targeting a city service for expanding your business is to identify a feasible city contracting out many services. This city is probably amenable to contracting for other services. Suppose Abilene contracts for many services but not your specialty, nurseries and grounds, for example. Your task is to apply your knowledge of nurseries and of Abilene decision makers and decision processes to the city's groundskeeping needs.

You may be lucky enough to be in a city that obviously needs the service you can provide. But if not, some adaptation is called for. The above outlines the major processes. The case histories in the preceding chapters enrich our understanding of the needed strategy. We now consider the parties to public service decisions and their goals and interests.

PARTIES TO PUBLIC DECISIONS AND INTERESTS OF EACH PARTY

Main parties to alternate delivery decisions at the local level are clients and citizens (indirectly but ultimately), elected officials, public managers, and public employees. Clients (users of services) want effective service (timely, customized to individual needs, knowledgeable and friendly personnel) at the least available cost. Service will be judged satisfactory or not based largely on expectations built on recent experience. Unless conditioned to expect otherwise, recipients of services and benefits will be willing to pay what they decide is a fair price for what they receive.

The main types of questions clients will have concerning alternate delivery of services are:

- Will the service still be as "good"?
- Will the hours or locations change?
- Will the personnel, their training, and friendliness change?
- Will the service be locally run or administered by some company away from here?
- Will the service continue or be considered expendable?

Citizens other than direct service recipients may be activists wanting a full range of services, or they may be passive except when voting. It is obviously important to entrepreneurs to determine citizens' sentiments on cost versus effectiveness. The trend in recent years has supposedly all been to lower costs. Yet there are interesting contrary signs. In July 1986 a large poll of Texans revealed that, in the face of severe delines in oil-based government revenues, they still wanted services maintained, even if tax rates had to be raised. One should not assume citizens only want lower taxes. Citizens will ask:

- Will service drop below acceptable levels?
- How will costs be lowered?
- Will training and skill of employees fall?

Elected government officials generally reflect politically active citizens' sentiments on cost versus services, since they are elected by those citizens. Yet officials also are sensitive to managers and employees. Officials of governments will then ask the same questions as citizens, clients, managers, and employees.

Managers and employees may be assumed to be more interested in effectiveness and expansion than in cost control. Managers' pay is usually correlated with the size of their budgets and staffs. Reasonably, more responsibility should be associated with more pay. The fallacy here is that more responsibility should refer to performance output, when in fact it often equals size of budget and staff (input).

Managers of government departments will ask:

• What will happen to our jobs?
• Will administering the contract and monitoring performance mean job security and advancement opportunities?
• Will performance and budget pressures increase?

There is increasing recognition of the need for education of public officials who set public managers' compensation on how to reward optimal perform- ance, whether delivered by city employees, through contracting out, franchises, or another arrangement. In the meantime the entrepreneur who acts on present realities will win the prize.

Employees of local government are, quite reasonably, interested in maintain- ing current income and current job environments. If unionized, then their clout is increased by central union office expertise and the union local's threat. They are also concerned about the level of service clients receive and about scandals in contracting, budgets, and other issues. But reasonably, employees are expected to give their personal well-being high priority. We know that imminent change threatens any of us who might be affected. Thus public employees' questions will be:

• Will we have jobs?
• How will our status change?
• Might we be reassigned?
• How will the new employer cut costs?
• What happens if performance standards are raised?
• Will there be competition for jobs?
• Will there be competition for raises?

SELLING ALTERNATE DELIVERY OF SERVICES

We now have an overview of the main targets—their concerns and the questions they can be expected to have. To become an expert on these decision makers, their goals, and their probable questions, the privatizer can participate in local politics, attend city council meetings, and develop a network of contacts through appropriate clubs and organizations. Particularly helpful will be city officials, contractors and franchisees to other cities, accounting firms, and management consultants. A less direct means is to attend seminars on public service delivery topics, city planning, financing, labor relations, and other city administration problems. The best single fact you can command is knowing where your kind of service has been successfully privatized. Best sources are likely to be publications of the Local Government Center, the International City Management Association, *American City and County* magazine, *Urban Resources* journal, and *Privatization Review*. Bellush (1985) typifies useful sources of information.

Only after you know your targets well and can empathize with key ones are you ready to face the next set of tasks. These are educating your targets to the benefits of your ideas and then selling them on the benefits your company can provide.

How can the entrepreneur overcome fear of a city official or managers who has not used a private employer for X service? A two-stage effort is called for: first, education about potential advantages of alternate service delivery, and second, information on the benefits of your particular firm as a supplier. This model has similarities but is distinct from Ferris and Grady's two-stage model of the decision to contract out (1986).

The task in *stage one* is to show advantages of private service delivery. The privatization problem at stage one is similar to that described in marketing as how to create primary demand for a type of product or service, as opposed to demand for a specific brand (Schoell, 1985). Comparison may be made with the phonograph company that brings out a compact disk (CD) and player. First the company must get people interested in CD's potential, show people it works, that it sounds much better, and is dependable. The entrepreneur seeking to introduce a private service alternative is about where Sony Corporation was when it developed the first videocassette recorder, Betamax. Pioneering—educating decision makers—through public relations and personal selling are called for. Stage one is executed by case information, cited from other cities' experience. (Forget theoretical arguments unless you are talking to a Ph.D. economist.) The entrepreneur should get detailed information—from phone calls and visits—after narrowing down to two or three successful cases. These should be as similar and geographically as close as possible to your target.

Stage two is the building of confidence in your particular company, starting with you, the leader, then presenting your company. Main questions to ask yourself are:

• Who will recommend you?

• What is your prior job and management experience?

• What contract successes have you or your company had recently?

• What is your company size, age, stability, and capability?

Of course, you must plan ways to ease any hurt to existing public employees in the transition from public to good business. Hiring city employees, for example, addresses this difficulty. One practical tactic that may be helpful is to hire a key employee of the city before the persuasion stages. Ideally you locate a person highly respected by city officials and management. This might be a person who is upwardly mobile and feels his or her promotions within city employment are blocked. This person then becomes a key communicator not only because he or she understands the city's needs but because he or she can help tailor the company's service to those needs.

TIMING AND SUMMARY

The preacher said in Ecclesiastes, "To everything there is a season." What times are best for an entrepreneur to expand into a heretofore public arena? One propitious time is at a change in administrations, that is, after officials are confident in their new posts but before they commit to plans, programs, budgets, and bureaucrats. Another key time is when there is serious, vocalized dissatisfaction with existing service delivery.

A third opportune time is based on the behavior of other cities. Across the country, private service delivery is apparently growing. One advantageous time for privatizing a delivery of service is soon after another city, admired by leaders in your city, makes its move. The Rochester, New York, experiences beginning in 1974 illustrate these three facets of privatization timing.

In conclusion, if the entrepreneur wants to help privatize local services by converting them to business for his company, a multistep process is in order. First is education about forces affecting choices of alternate delivery of services. Second is knowing the decision makers, their concerns, and questions. Third is building interest and even demand for alternate service providers. And fourth is positioning one's own company to fill that demand. Trend watcher John Naisbitt, author of *Megatrends* and coauthor of *Reinventing the Corporation* (1985) observes that entrepreneurial companies are assuming more responsibility for a variety of services in the United States. Given careful attention by entrepreneurs, this trend should continue.

REFERENCES

Abell, Derek F., and Hammond, John S. (1979). *Strategic Market Planning*. Englewood Cliffs, NJ: Prentice-Hall.

Bellush, S. M. (1985, October) "Private Choice," *American City and County*, pp. 62-65.

Caves, D. W., and Christensen, L. R. (1980, October). "The Relative Efficiency of Public and Private Firms in a Competitive Environment: The Case of Canadian Railroads," *Journal of Political Economy*, 88, no. 5, 958-976.

Caves, D. W., Christensen, L. R., and Swanson, J. A. (1981, November). "Economic

˙Performance in Regulated and Unregulated Environments: A Comparison of U.S. and Canadian Railroads," *The Quarterly Journal of Economics*, 9, no. 4, 559-581.

Ferris, J., and Graddy, E. (1986, July/August) "Contracting Out: ·For What? With Whom?" *Public Administration Review* 46, no. 4, 332-344.

Finley, L. (1987, winter) "An Entrepreneurial Process for Privatization at the Local Level," *The Privatization Review*, 3, no. 19-25.

Finley, L. (1984, summer) "Can Your Small Company Acquire Resources as Favorably as the Large Company?" *American Journal of Small Business*, 9, no. 1, 19-25.

Herbert, R. F., and Link, A. N. (1982). *The Entrepreneur, Mainstream Views and Radical Critiques*. New York: Praeger.

Naisbitt, J., and Aburdene, P. (1985). *Reinventing the Corporation*. New York: Warner Books.

Pescatrice, D. R., and Trapani, J. M., III. (1980, April) "The Performance and Objectives of Public and Private Utilities Operating in the United States," *Journal of Public Economics*, 13, 259-276.

Porter, M. E. (1980). *Competitive Strategy*. New York: Macmillan.

Schoell, William F. (1985). *Marketing: Contemporary Concepts and Practices*, 2d ed. Boston: Allyn & Bacon.

Touche Ross and Co. (1985). *Financing Infrastructure in America*. Chicago: Touche Ross.

12

Privatization in Europe

JAN PIETER VAN OUDENHOVEN

Privatization is currently fashionable in Europe. (When referring to Europe or European countries, we are referring to Western European countries exclusively.) Without exception, the European countries are beginning to realize that the state should reduce its role in the economy. This is not surprising. Taxes, as a percentage of the gross domestic product (GDP), have increased from an average of 36 percent in 1976 to an average of 40 percent in 1986 in the Western European countries. All countries, including Spain with its socialist government, have their privatization programs. The most radical programs may be found in Turkey, the United Kingdom, and France, where the socialists lost their majority in 1986. Generally, the privatization programs have the following objectives:

1. reduction of the collective expenditure in order to allow more room for private investment;
2. enhancement of the efficiency of the government apparatus by the discipline of the market mechanism;
3. reinforcement of competition in order to stimulate innovations.

It is reasonable to assume that these objectives are economically sound and that privatization is a good means to reach them. In fact, most economists subscribe to this assumption. However, there are two problems with the realization of these objectives. First, for most governments, privatization has become a goal in itself instead of a means. Second, although there are many ways to reduce government influence upon socioeconomic life, privatization has primarily taken the form of denationalization, that is, the partial or total sale of state enterprises to the private sector. This method of privatization is relatively easy and garners a lot of publicity. However, it is doubtful whether denationalization will reduce the collective expenditure or the general tax level. There seems to be no direct relation between a country's level of taxes and the degree of state involvement in the national economy. Even the inverse may be true: Of all twenty-three countries in the Organization for Cooperation and Economic Development (OECD), Turkey, for instance, has the lowest tax (17 percent) as a percentage of its GDP, while the Turkish state, with its 263 state enterprises, controls approximately half of the national economy. The Netherlands, on the other hand, has the lowest percentage of state-owned enterprises in Europe but has one of the highest tax levels (46 percent) in Europe.

In addition to the three objectives mentioned above, some governments also aim to spread private share ownership. France and the United Kingdom have been very successful in this objective. Since December 1986, the number of private shareholders in France has increased from 2 million to approximately 6 million. In Britain, the number of private shareholders has more than tripled since 1979, when Margaret Thatcher took office. In 1987 there were approximately 9 million shareholders in Britain, which is more than one-fifth of the adult population. These shareholders will probably vote Conservative, as renationalization programs of the Labour party in Great Britain or the Socialist party in France might threaten the value of their equities. This may be one of the reasons why Conservative governments are such staunch supporters of denationalization programs.

The next four sections discuss the divergent privatization experiences in four countries: United Kingdom, France, West Germany, and the Netherlands.

UNITED KINGDOM

The privatization versus nationalization debate has always been very intense in Britain because of the two-party electoral competition leading to the so-called "pendulum" effect: the socialists attempting to expand the public sector and the conservatives, on the other hand, aiming to reduce it. Nevertheless, the actual privatizations by former Conservative administrations were only marginal. However, since the election of Margaret Thatcher in 1979 the Conservative policy has changed dramatically, as we are by now all aware. Actually, it was time for something to happen in the ailing British economy. On the national scale, public enterprises were doing worse than the private companies (Pryke, 1982), but international comparisons also showed that British nationalized industries were at a disadvantage. One of the major problems of the British state enterprises was their lack of autonomy. They were used for political purposes by both Labour and Conservative governments. At the time the enterprises were used to restrain inflation, or they were sometimes pressured to merge with, or to take over, other companies in order to save jobs.

At the same time they were not allowed to concentrate or diversify their actions toward more profitable regions. Their investments were largely reduced by strict external financing limits, which were primarily based upon political considerations. In addition, state enterprises were not allowed to carry out their own personnel policies and were often required to keep superfluous personnel employed, particularly in troubled sectors or regions.

During two parliaments the Thatcher administration has reduced the proportion of GDP in the hands of state industries from 10.5 to approximately 6.5 percent. In this same period more than 600,000 jobs have been transferred to the private sector "to liberate economic activity from suffocation by the State," according to the Thatcher administration. Not all would agree with this statement. A common criticism is that Thatcher is selling off state properties. Indeed, some lucrative public sector assets were sold at extremely low prices, as recent flotations of British Airways and Rolls Royce show. The share price of British Airways soared to an immediate premium of 84 percent; the premium of Rolls Royce was 70 percent. However, before offering further evaluations of the British privatization program, we will discuss the denationalization of British Telecom (BT) and British Petroleum (BP), as these two cases are good illustrations of the recent privatization policy.

British Telecom

BT (privatized for 51 percent in 1984) was not only the greatest but also the most complicated transfer of a public industry to the private sector in the first five years of the Thatcher government. Earlier denationalizations primarily involved companies that were already in competition with private enterprises. BT was, and still is, a natural monopoly as far as the network facilities are concerned. This is logical, since the duplication of complete networks would be highly inefficient, and the supplier with many subscribers has a big advantage over suppliers with only a relatively small number of subscribers. The government did little to stimulate competition. On the contrary, it limited the liberalization in order to enhance the likelihood of a successful sale. Only Mercury, a subsidiary of Cable and Wireless, received a license to run a telecommunication network, but this company, with a market of no more than 1 or 2 percent, will never constitute a severe threat to BT. Moreover, no other company will be allowed to compete until November 1990. These measures coupled with the massive advertising campaign helped to sell the 3 billion shares (51 percent of the company), but what probably prompted most sales was the low price: 130p per share, payable in three installments. In the first week after its introduction on the stockmarket a 50p share (the first part of the installment) was traded at a price of 90 to 92.5p, and its real value has increased much more since.

Was the privatization of BT a success? For the government it was. It raised nearly £4 billion, but it could have received much more. Would any private company sell its assets at such a low price? It is highly unlikely. Nor did the privatization lead to more competition. Instead of being a state-owned monopoly, BT now is a privately owned monopoly. The new shareholders have reason to be content, since BT's near-monopoly position is the best guarantee that their investment is safe. Apparently privatization and competition do not necessarily go hand in hand. Actually, it would have been much easier to liberalize BT if it were still a state enterprise, or as Vickers and Yarrow (1986) note, "In any industry, the time to restructure is before privatisation." The privatization of BT did not enhance the management efficiency either, for a privatized monopoly requires even more regulations than a state monopoly. It is common knowledge that BT's service has deteriorated since privatization. Safe in the private sector, it has few incentives to meet the criticisms about the poor state of public telephone booths, slow repairs, and late installations.

British Petroleum

"BP: be part of it" was the slogan of the best organized privatization campaign in Great Britain. "BP: be no part of it" was The Observer's advice a few days before BP's offer expired. What was intended to be the most successful sale turned out to be the greatest flop. What happened?

The British government launched its biggest share sale of £7.2 billion in October 1987. The BP offer was divided into two chunks: a fixed-price offer for private British investors, and an international offer for institutions and overseas buyers. The government set the fixed price at £3.30, which represented a 6 percent discount on the previous day's closing price. Buyers would pay for the stock in three installments. The first was due on purchase; the second in August 1988, and the third in April 1989. Six million people had expressed interest in the issue, but then the October crash came, and the price plunged to £2.50. Only 270,000 of the 6 million potential private investors finally applied for shares. Fortunately for the government, British and foreign investment banks had formally agreed to guarantee the issue for a fee. They were forced to accept the shares at a huge loss. However, to remove any further downside risk, the Bank of England offered a floor price to buy back each of the new partly paid BP shares. Several newspaper comments said that this was the first privatization with a built-in renationalization.

BP had been operating for decades in competition with other oil companies, so that further privatization was not needed in order to enhance its competitiveness. A more down-to-earth objective was to obtain money for the treasury's coffers. The government got its money, but at the expense of huge financial losses for the participating investment banks, which will be much more reluctant to get involved in future flotations. A more political goal was to promote the spread of private share ownership. A large, expensive propaganda campaign persuaded more than 6 million British citizens to register their interest in the offer, but the stock market crash prevented 95 percent of them from applying. Of course, the government cannot be blamed for failure to foresee the crash. Yet it should have realized that public support of the privatization program is largely dependent upon the favorable price developments in the stock market.

General Conclusions about the British Privatization Program

The BT case shows that privatization offers no guarantee for competition, since BT continues to operate as a monopoly. The state might have been better off using its influence to stimulate competition. On the other hand, BP has always been efficiently operated in full competition with other oil companies. Moreover, it had already been largely privatized for several years. What could the motives be for the further privatization of an efficiently run profit-making enterprise? The first is to obtain money for the treasury as a means of reducing the government's budget deficit. This, however, is a very short-sighted policy, since only the profitable companies can be sold. Unprofitable companies have to be given away or remain in the hands of the state. Besides, the high flotation costs reduce the one-time positive effect to the treasury. The second motive—primarily an ideological one—is to spread the share ownership in order to involve more people in the market process. Before the privatization of BP, the Thatcher administration had been very successful in fulfilling this objective. Ironically, the money spent in the flotation campaign amounted to more than just giving away the BP shares to the few private persons that actually bought some would have cost. That is the lesson to be learned from the BP case: privatization will receive public support only as long as the stock market cooperates.

In terms of the objectives mentioned in the introduction, the British privatization program has only been moderately successful. (1) The government's stake in the national enterprises has been reduced considerably, but it is primarily the profitable ones that have been sold. (2) Some of the privatized firms, for example, National Freight Corporation and Jaguar, are undoubtedly better run than under state ownership. However, the recent general criticism of BT warns against converting public monopolies into private monopolies. (3) Enhancing competition no longer seems to constitute an important motive. BT has not changed its monopoly status, and BP was already a totally competitive enterprise. (4) The government has been very successful in spreading the share ownership among private investors, so that even the Labour party is hesitant to renationalize the privatized enterprises.

Probably the best outcome of the privatization program is that it has stimulated a popular interest in economics and a revival of entrepreneurship. Some state enterprises, for instance, particularly British Steel, are now operating more commercially. The private interest in investing in the Channel Tunnel is another example of this enterprising attitude.

Aside from the Labour party and the trade unions, which have always been opposed to any privatization, there has been a lot of criticism of the British privatization policy. In spite of serious objections—even by conservative economists—the Thatcher administration continues with its privatization without indicating much willingness to take into account some of the suggestions made by its critics. Social psychologists would call this a very clear example of "group think": the phenomenon that a very cohesive group sticks to its own decisions and defends itself against criticism from the outside while the group members—the dissidents have disappeared—reinforce one another and interpret outside criticism as evidence of their being right.

FRANCE

As in Britain, nationalizations and privatizations in France have been largely ideological in nature. The 1980s witnessed a spectacular growth of the public sector when the socialists were in power, but also an equally spectacular privatization program since the conservatives won the elections in 1987. In contrast with Britain, public enterprises in France have always been rather competitive and have always possessed greater freedom to acquire subsidiaries and to diversify into other fields. In fact, because of this freedom, French public enterprises have been able to take over and thus "silently" nationalize hundreds of companies.

In addition to this gradual process of nationalization the socialists expanded the public sector in an unequaled way during the initial years of the socialist government (Parris, Pestieau, and Saynor, 1987). The proportion of the public sector in undertakings with more than 2,000 employees rose from 15.8 to 41 percent. The increase was especially dramatic in three sectors: iron, steel, minerals, and metals, from 4.3 to 35.6 percent; mechanical and electrical, from 9.7 to 23.7 percent; and chemicals, glass, and pharmaceuticals, from 10.6 to 27.3 percent. The thirty-nine banks nationalized in 1982 owned about 90 percent of all demand deposits and liquid investments. The state also intervened more often than before in industrial groups that were in serious financial difficulties. Striking was the public investment in technologically advanced sectors. The high-technology firms had to be held under national control. One of the consequences of this policy is that the state now has a very strong foothold in the electronics industry, particularly after the takeover of Thomson.

In comparing the French public sector with the British public sector we can distinguish three main differences. First, it is much larger, even in comparison with the pre-Thatcher public sector. Second, it is more involved in high technology, such as nuclear energy, electronics, aerospace, and pharmaceuticals. Third, state enterprises compete to a great extent with private firms. On the whole the nationalized industries increased their sales and some newly formed industries succeeded in eliminating losses and even started to make profits.

After 1982, with the socialists still in power, there were no new nationalizations, not even of private concerns with major financial problems, which elsewhere in Europe would have been sufficient reason for nationalization. New elections, in March 1986, brought a conservative coalition to power. A year and a half later twenty-three enterprises had been resold to the private sector for a total sum of 100 billion francs (about $17 billion). The aims of Edouard Balladur, the French minister of finance, were to promote "popular capitalism," to get employees more involved in their own firms, and to make the French economy more competitive. He has been quite successful in realizing these aims, particularly in spreading share ownership: within one year the number of private shareowners has increased from 2 million to 6 million, which is not surprising considering that privatized shares were, on the average, 17 percent more profitable than other shares traded on the Paris stock market. Unfortunately for the minister of finance, one black Monday on the stock market in October 1987 did more damage to his privatization program than all socialist efforts could do.

A typically French invention is the so-called *noyau dur* (hard core). We will briefly describe these *noyaux durs* and we will, as in the case of Britain, give two illustrations of privatizations: Saint Gobain and Compagnie Financière de Suez.

The *noyaux durs*, groups of shareholders selected by the minister of finance in consultation with the enterprises concerned, are meant to protect the newly privatized firms from raiders or foreign takeovers. These *noyaux durs*, which together usually dispose of 20 to 30 percent of the shares, are obliged to hold their shares for several years in order to make it possible for the privatized companies to reorganize themselves and consolidate their partnerships. Although the *noyaux durs* policy seems to be reasonable, it has constituted the most criticized part of the French privatization program. Even the Liberal party, one of the coalition partners, reproached the government for forming cliques in the French economy.

Saint Gobain

Saint Gobain, the glass manufacturer, nationalized in 1982, was the first enterprise to be reprivatized. It was a rather easy privatization, since the company had always been in full competition and had, in fact, been a private firm most of the time. It was also a pleasant privatization, both for the bank and the new shareholders. The bank that sold Saint Gobain to the public received a large fee. Shareholders saw the shares increase 20 percent above their offer price when trading opened, and they saw the share value climb from the FFr 310 offer price to almost FFr 500 within a year. The first shareholders' meeting after privatization attracted so many new shareowners that it had to be held in a huge Parisian concert hall. Finally, in spite of the criticism on the underpricing, it was a success for the government as well, since the Saint

Gobain case showed that small investors could be interested in buying state assets. Popular capitalism proved to be viable.

Compagnie Financière de Suez

Founded in 1858 by Ferdinand de Lesseps as a company to exploit the Suez Canal, the Compagnie Financière de Suez (or more simply Suez) did not receive its actual name until a century later, two years after President Nasser of Egypt nationalized the Suez Canal. The new company decided to invest its reserves of FFr 5 billion in three activities: banking, industry, and liquid investments. Within ten years it became one of the leading French financing companies. In 1982 the Suez group was nationalized. Apparently the nationalization did not impede growth: From 1982 to 1986 the number of companies integrated in the Suez group increased from 78 to 182; the number of employees went from 10,770 to 17,600; in four years the balance increased from FFr 197 to 333 billion; and the net profit during 1986 amounted to FFr 2.4 billion as compared to FFr 445 million in 1982. Yet, according to Renaud de la Beniere (*Le Monde*, October 21, 1987), currently president of Suez, privatization is necessary to give the state enterprises back to the logic of the market, which is not national any more, nor European, but worldwide.

Suez, or more precisely 80 percent of its 61 million shares, was given back to the market on October 5, 1987, at a price of FFr 317 a share. The private investors took 30 percent, 28 percent went to the *noyau dur*, 10 percent to the employees, and the rest to foreign investors. This time the *noyau dur* consisted of four industrial companies with which the Suez group wanted to strengthen its relationships, nine French financial institutions, and ten foreign investment groups. Two weeks after the offer the stock market collapsed, leading to an extremely low first Suez quotation of FFr 261 in November instead of the FFr 380-390 predicted by brokers a month earlier. In order to reduce the disappointment for the 1.6 million small investors and the nearly 18,000 employees, the government allowed them to pay for the shares in two installments. This was actually not fair to the shareholders of the previously privatized companies, since they had equal reasons to be disappointed by the share prices fallback. In spite of this measure the new Suez shareholders were very disappointed and even feared more severe losses, which is probably why 2 million shares were sold on the first quotation day.

Suez is back in the private sector. It owes its existence and its reputation to private initiative. There were no sound economic reasons to nationalize the group; it was primarily a political decision. Nevertheless, Suez operated quite well as a public enterprise. There were no urgent economic reasons to privatize the company, at least not in the radical way in which it was done. The nationalization and privatization of Suez—both primarily political actions—have cost a lot of energy and money, which could have been spent more productively to improve the French economy.

General Conclusions about the French
Privatization Program

No other country has known as many fluctuations in nationalizations and privatizations as France. After the elections of 1981, the socialists nationalized enterprises on an unprecedented scale in the economic history of Western countries. When the conservatives won the elections five years later, their reaction was no less radical: within one year, twenty-three enterprises representing capital of more than FFr 100 billion were sold to the private sector. It took the conservative coalition only one year to realize a third of its privatization program. While the privatized enterprises have barely had sufficient time to reorganize themselves in accordance with the new political situation, the privatization program has become considerably less popular since the stock market crash.

The French economy seems to have a double handicap. In addition to the general economic malaise, it is faced with the permanent threat of political interventions, whether these be nationalizations or privatizations. Fortunately most enterprises have survived these interventions, including the nationalizations, and are functioning quite well, thanks to their generally competitive attitude. In France the privatization versus nationalization controversy has become a political intergroup conflict rather than an economic issue. Instead of economic arguments such wartime language as "saving one's face," "combatting the public sector," or "the defeat of the privatization program" are used. Moreover, the privatization campaign is receiving notorious publicity, which causes the intergroup conflict to escalate even more. Against the background of this ideological warfare, the French industry must struggle to keep its continuity. In Britain the privatization issue has also been largely ideological, but there were more economic arguments to privatize the public sector. Another difference between France and Britain is that in the latter there has been more political continuity with regard to the privatization policy. In the 1970s the actual policy differences between Labour and Conservative administrations were of minor importance, and since the time that Margaret Thatcher took office in 1979, the privatization message has always been clear and constant.

French state enterprises are hardly less efficient than private enterprises. Besides, they usually operate in full competition with other companies. This may be the reason that, in promoting its privatization program, the French government has perhaps stressed too much the importance of "popular capitalism," that is, the participation of small investors in the stock market. There are many ways in which to privatize public enterprises. The reservation of large percentages of shares for private investors is a political decision that attracts a lot of favorable publicity as long as the stock market cooperates. However, if the market falls, as it did in 1987, publicity may change accordingly, and public interest may also collapse. The dependence of the program's success on the stock market makes it very vulnerable. Perhaps some adjustments in the direction of the German program should be the goal. Germany's policy will be discussed in the next section.

FEDERAL REPUBLIC OF GERMANY

West Germany has a considerable public sector, which is largely an inheritance of the Nazi period when the state penetrated all sectors of society. The public enterprise sector has a share of more than 10 percent in the GDP. The state is particularly represented in the finance and credit branch; public banks hold more than 50 percent of the total of account balances of all banks. The public involvement is more complicated than in most other countries, since in addition to the state (federal level) the *Länder* (states) are active participants as well.

States enterprises in Germany possess great freedom. There is very little government supervision, and state enterprises are not used as a macroeconomic instrument at all (Parris et al., 1987). Public authorities in West Germany favor experts from the private sector of the economy to run their public enterprises. Not surprisingly, the enterprises are allowed to have their own personnel policies (with the exception of the Deutsche Bundespost and the Bundesbahn, the national railway company) and are given free reign in their investments.

In sharp contrast with Great Britain and France, there has never been a significant controversy between the main political parties in Germany about the nationalization versus privatization issue. On the contrary, between the Christian Democrats and the Social Democrats there is a strong consensus that no concentration of economic power should develop in the hands of the state. Even during the period from 1969 to 1982, when the Social Democrats were the dominant partner in the coalition with the Free Democrats, no appreciable extension of the public sector took place. This liberal attitude may be explained as a reaction to the trauma of the Nazi regime when the state was interfering in all sectors of society. Interestingly, one of the strongest actions against the recent privatization plans has been Franz Joseph Strauss's successful opposition to the privatization of Lufthansa. Strauss, the powerful Christian Democrat prime minister of Bavaria and at the same time the government representative at Airbus industries, was afraid that a privatized Lufthansa might change its aircraft acquisition plans (Uhel, 1986).

On the whole, the German "program of reduction of federal participation," as the privatization program is officially called, has been rather pragmatic. Stability of the financial market and continuity of the enterprises' management have always been more important than ideological arguments. In spite of the generally favorable attitude toward it, the privatization program is rather modest and is being carried out at a very slow pace. It took the government several years to decide which enterprises would be privatized, and not until 1986 did it decide to privatize five companies instead of eleven as it had originally planned. Four of the companies to be privatized are rather small, with turnovers between DM 350 and 600 million. Besides, the privatizations are only partial; the state will hold from 25 to 60 percent of ownership. Before 1986 the government took two concrete steps toward privatization: a reduction of its stakes in VEBA and Volkswagen. Both cases will be discussed briefly, since they provide good illustrations of the cautious way in which the Germans privatize.

VEBA

VEBA is a broadly based industrial and service organization specializing in electricity generation and supply, oil and gas, chemicals, and trading and transport. Its total external sales amounted to more than DM 40 billion in 1986, with a group net profit of DM 1.020 billion. In 1965 the state had already sold 57 percent of its shares. In May 1983 the cabinet decided to reduce the federal participation in VEBA from 43 to 30 percent. This second partial privatization of VEBA, which took place in January 1984, was carried out on the financial market through the medium of banks; they had to give a preferential treatment to German subscribers. Though there was a discount for private investors, the quotation was too high to be attractive for small investors. In 1985 the state reduced its involvement in VEBA even further, this time from 30 to 25.7 percent. This reduction took place when the state did not participate in the augmentation of the capital. As is typical of Germany's privatization policy, state participation is still sufficient to guarantee veto power to the government. In this sense privatizations in Germany are only partial.

Volkswagen

Volkswagen is Germany's second biggest enterprise with a turnover (1986) of DM 53 billion and a net profit of DM 580 million. In 1961 the government had already sold 60 percent of the Volkswagen shares; the remaining shares remained in the hands of the federal government and the *land* (state) government of Lower Saxony, each with 20 percent. In 1961 promoting capitalism was an important objective. The sale was therefore not carried out via the stock market. Instead there was a preferential offer for private subscribers, a fixed number of shares for the investors (ten for employees and five for the other subscribers), and payments to be made in installments. In addition, the buyers had to hold the shares for a period of time. However, fiscal fraud and underpricing were the reasons that this form was no longer used for later privatizations.

A nice illustration of German slowness (prudence?) is the subsequent privatization process of Volkswagen. From September 1985 until the summer of 1986, state participation was reduced to 16 percent by a nonparticipation of the government in the augmentation of the capital. A sale of the remaining federal shares, due to take place in November 1987, was postponed because of the sharp fall of share values the month before. They were finally sold in March 1988.

Concluding Remarks about the German
Privatization Program

Although the two big political parties in Germany agree that the state's involvement in the economic sector should be at the lowest possible level, the privatization of the considerable public sector is being carried out at a very slow pace. The need for privatization is not so intensely apparent, probably because the federal government's attitude toward state enterprises has been very liberal since 1945. In Germany privatization is primarily an economic issue, not a political one. Economically, there is not much difference between private and public enterprises. That is probably why the German press does not pay much attention to the privatization issue; articles on privatization in the German papers tend to refer to the British and French programs rather than to their own. In Britain or France, on the other hand, each privatization program is extensively commented upon in the national press and is usually interpreted in terms of winning or losing for the ruling party. Any delay in the privatization program is seen as "losing face" for the British and French governments, even under the present unfavorable stock market circumstances. On the contrary, in Germany under the present circumstances, a delay in the program is considered a wise reaction to a changing economic situation. The Dutch program, which will be discussed in the next section, is similar to the German privatization policy.

THE NETHERLANDS

The Netherlands has known a long tradition of private initiative. Even the great colonialization in the seventeenth century was financed by a limited liability company. Several centuries later, after the French occupation by Napoleon, King Willem I used his own capital to breathe life into the dying national economy. He founded a trading company that became, after it merged with a bank, the most important commercial bank in the Netherlands, the Algemene Bank Nederland.

In line with this tradition of private initiative, the public sector in the Netherlands—only 3.6 percent of the GDP—is smaller than in any other European country. The nationalization of industries has never been a political aim for any of the three big political parties (Social Democrats, Christian Democrats, and Liberals). State enterprises do not suffer from government interference and, aside from the PTT (the national post and telephone company), possess a large degree of independence. At times the government has participated in floundering companies (for example, shipbuilding concerns) in order to save employment, and at other times for more strategic reasons such as its recent (December 1987) 49 percent participation in the Fokker Aircraft Company. In general, the Dutch government approach toward nationalization and privatization has been rather reserved and pragmatic.

In spite of the fact that the Dutch public sector is quite small, the government wants to privatize this sector even more and has been doing so for the past few years. However, as is the case with Germany, the privatization pace is rather slow: In 1987 the most important action was the reduction of state participation in the Nederlandsche Middenstandsbank, the fourth largest commercial bank in the Netherlands, from 14 (22 percent in 1985) to 7 percent. More important was the merger in 1986 of the Postal Cheque and Giro Services with the State Post Savings Bank and its transformation into the Post Bank, a bank with private law status that nevertheless remains completely state-owned. The Post Bank is now operating in full competition with private banks and is able to grant loans to businesses. Even more important will be the transformation of PTT into a company with private law status, a change scheduled to take place in January 1989. By that time the government will end the PTT's monopoly on telephone equipment and will encourage competition with regard to digital peripheral equipment. Anticipating these measures, PTT has already liberalized the sale of telephone equipment. However, the PTT will continue to have a monopoly on public telegraph, telephone, telex, and data transmission services.

In the next section two privatization cases will be discussed: KLM (Royal Dutch Airlines), and DSM (Dutch State Mines), which the government wants to privatize in 1988.

KLM

KLM is sixth on the world list of major airlines. In addition to passengers, it also transports a considerable amount of freight. After a number of meagre years the company has become profitable again, with average profits of more than $150 million over the last five years.

In most countries there is at least one (partially) state-owned airline. KLM is the Dutch national air company. The most important reason for state participation is that landing rights usually have to be acquired through bilateral negotiations between governments. State participation in KLM has been considerably reduced in recent years. The reduction of the state holding occurred rather inadvertently. In 1984 the first reduction took place, from 78 to 55 percent, partly through the sale of shares, partly by a share issue in which the government did not participate. In 1986 the government's stake in KLM was further reduced to 39 percent. However, this percentage is enough to hold the option to retrieve the majority of the shares at any time it wishes to do so. Besides, the government still retains the right to appoint half of the board members plus one, but aside from that does not intervene at all in the management of the company.

KLM has been largely privatized, but the company's policies have not changed. It makes little difference to the company whether the state has a majority or a minority holding. KLM has always been an enterprise in full competition with other airlines. It has been profitable for several years, even before the first reduction in state participation took place, so that one may wonder whether any further privatization of KLM would be wise.

Dutch States Mines

Dutch State Mines (DSM), established as a company in 1902 in order to exploit coal mines, closed its last mine in 1965. After its transformation into a chemical company, DSM has now become a concern that operates internationally with some 27,000 employees. Its turnover amounted to $10 billion in 1986 and its profits to well over $200 million. Although the state owns 100 percent of the shares, DSM has been completely managed as a private enterprise since 1966, when it was converted into a state-owned company with private law status. Not surprisingly, DSM has been a candidate for privatization ever since privatization in Europe became fashionable. In August 1987, when the Dutch cabinet decided to privatize DSM, the stock market value was estimated at approximately $6 billion. Some 30 percent of the shares are due to be sold in 1988. Reactions of DSM management are generally favorable, since a privatized DSM will be able to issue new shares on the stock market in order to finance its huge research program. Moreover, joint ventures will be facilitated by the possibility of exchanging shares. The company's only fear is that it might be taken over, but that seems to be a minor objection that can be overcome by spreading the shares or by retaining a substantial government holding.

Concluding Remarks on the Dutch Privatization Program

There are relatively few public enterprises in the Netherlands; their share of the national economy is relatively small; and they are rather independent in their management. Major state enterprises are PTT, Dutch Railways, the National Bank, Postbank, and DSM. With the exception of the Dutch Railways, all these companies are profitable; thus privatization of public enterprises in the Netherlands does not seem to be urgent. Nevertheless, a privatization program does exist: DSM will be at least partially privatized in the coming years, the PTT will receive private law status in 1989, and some minor companies will be transferred to the private sector.

PRIVATIZATION IN EUROPE: GENERAL CONCLUSIONS

The 1980s may be called the decade of the market mechanism. In all Western European countries—and in other regions as well—governments are attempting to reduce the role of the state in their national economies. Ambitious privatization programs, aimed at transferring state enterprises to the private sector are currently in progress, as in Britain and France, or are about to be implemented, as in Austria, Turkey, and Portugal. Except for the Netherlands with its small number of public enterprises all European countries still have many state enterprises that could easily be run as private enterprises.

A state enterprise that can turn losses into profits by being privatized should be privatized. This is an economic argument. However, if a state-owned company is as profitable and run as efficiently as it would be under private conditions, then whether it should be privatized or not is a matter of ideology. In the literature about privatization, economic and ideological arguments are usually interwined. It is difficult to give purely economic reasons why private enterprises would be a better bet than state enterprises. In order to find out which sort of enterprise is more efficient, comparisons are required between private and state undertakings that are in competition and engaged in the same type of business (Pryke, 1982). Methodologically sound field experiments are extremely difficult, since other important variables may covary with the kind of ownership (state or private). Thus, the alleged effect of the ownership variable might be attributed to the other variables as well. Admittedly, some serious comparative studies have been made, but unfortunately most of them were conducted in the United States. The United States experiences cannot easily be generalized to fit the European socioeconomic situation.

One major socioeconomic aspect that distinguishes Europe from the United States is the important role socialist parties play in political life. Most countries had, or still have, socialist governments or might end up with them again sooner or later. Their influence on the way economic life, including private enterprises, is organized has probably reduced the difference between private and state undertakings. Private enterprises are also subject to many social regulations. Moreover, when conservative and liberal political parties are in power, their actual policy does not differ all that much from socialist policy. The reason may be that they have to form a government with a more left-oriented coalition partner, or—more frequently—that the electorate would not accept a radical political switch. This may explain why most European privatization programs are rather cautious; in nearly all cases privatizations are only partial, with the state wanting to maintain a role in the privatized enterprises. Even "radical" Margaret Thatcher had to promise the electorate in the last elections not to denationalize the British National Health Service, which is the most expensive health system in Europe with expenditures amounting to approximately £14.5 billion a year and employees numbering roughly 1,250,000.

Has privatization had a positive influence on the European economy? This question is difficult to answer. Let us take Britain as an example. The Thatcher administration will certainly say that privatization has been very successful. Undertakings that have thus far been denationalized are all flourishing under private ownership. Productivity of the British nationalized sector was notoriously low in the 1970s, but the performance of British private industry was not much better. At present the private sector is also doing better, and even some state enterprises that were renowned loss makers are now generating profits. British Steel, for instance, which had chalked up losses totaling nearly £6 billion over eight years, made a remarkable turnaround with profits that totaled £178 million in 1986 and for 1987 were expected to increase to approximately £300 million. British Steel's turnaround has been achieved by drastic cuts in personnel, which have sufficiently reduced costs to make it one of the most efficient steelmakers in Europe. This has paved the way for privatization in the next few years. British Steel is a good illustration of European privatization policy. Privatization, it is said, is needed to make state enterprises (more) profitable, but state enterprises first have to be made profitable before they may be privatized.

Renault is a similar example. Nationalized in 1945 (because it collaborated with Nazi Germany), it has accumulated a debt to the state estimated at $10 billion. After a series of reductions in staff due to a drastic robotization, Renault has been made profitable again. The French goverment is now thinking of remitting $2 billion of Renault's debt and plans to privatize Renault in 1988. No wonder that privatized enterprises are doing better than state enterprises. However, the companies that are very difficult to make profitable, such as most railway companies, remain in the hands of the state.

Privatization is perhaps not the big engine of economic recovery that many economists and politicians contend. It may rather be just one consequence of a changing economic climate, perhaps the ideological finishing touch upon the changed economic climate. European industry was enveloped in a recession in the 1970s; it had lost its dynamics. For many enterprises—private or state-owned—keeping people employed became as important as, and sometimes even more important than, making profits. During the last decade it was once again fashionable to make profits. Both private and state-owned enterprises have become more efficient and competitive. Most enterprises have reduced their staff when that was necessary to increase their productivity. Many state enterprises in Europe that were suffering losses or were hardly profitable ten years ago are currently quite profitable. Thus one wonders why they should be privatized, if economic arguments are not decisive. The reasons may be ideological as they often are in Great Britain and France. Not surprisingly, in countries such as West Germany and the Netherlands where privatization is not such an ideological issue, privatization takes place at a very slow pace.

In addition to the economic and ideological reasons there are two additional motives for privatization. The first is to promote popular capitalism. We have seen that France and Britain have been very successful in attracting new groups of private investors. The other motive—equally important, but less frequently expressed officially—is to raise funds for the treasury, which can be used to reduce taxation or the deficit. However, selling state assets to raise funds has become less attractive since share prices on the stock market have fallen sharply. The fact that few privatization activities are currently taking place underlines the importance of the two motives just mentioned. Apparently the more economic motives for privatization, such as greater efficiency of the public sector, are not sufficiently compelling to continue with the program.

Most economic objects of privatization, such as efficiency enhancement, reinforcement of competition, and reduction of collective expenditure, are still valid. However, these objectives may also be fulfilled by state enterprises. When privatization came into fashion in the late 1970s, the anti-model was the British large-scale industrial corporation: inflexible, overcentralized, and overstaffed. Nowadays the distinction between private and state enterprises is blurred (Parris et al., 1987). Private companies are increasingly subjected to state influence when governments consider the national interest is at stake, as with companies supplying defense requirements or those engaged in high technology. On the other hand, there is a clear tendency for public enterprises to become more commercial.

Local Changes

For politicians, the privatization of state enterprises is a relatively pleasant measure. Essentially it is just a matter of selling state assets and receiving money in the bargain. It is doubtful whether privatization of state enterprises is the most useful strategy to reduce the state influence upon socioeconomic life in Europe. It might be wiser to focus on the transfer of public services—primarily provided by local governments—to the private sector. Plans are abundant; concrete actions are relatively scarce. Yet there are some promising activities going on. In Switzerland more than thirty municipalities have contracted out their police surveillance to a private enterprise. In some countries there exists a financial leasing system for infrastructural projects. In Belgium, for instance, local authorities may lease buildings. In any country, but especially in France, toll roads may be found. In the Netherlands a growing number of municipalities are contracting out garbage collection, generally at lower costs. Finally, we give an example of volunteer personnel in health care: in Amsterdam AIDS patients get nursing assistance and social support from volunteer "buddies."

Privatization of publicly delivered services at the local government level often requires creativity. Privatization at this level is probably a greater challenge for the genuine entrepreneur than privatization at the state level which usually involves political and formal actions. Until now most emphasis has been on the denationalization of state enterprises; it is time for European local government authorities to become local entrepreneurs.

REFERENCES

De Nederlandsche Bank (1986). *Annual Report.*
Parris, H., P. Pestieau, and P. Saynor (1987). *Public Enterprise in Western Europe.* London: Croom Helm.

Pryke, R. (1982). "The Comparative Performance of Public and Private Enterprise," *Fiscal Studies*, 3, no. 2, 68-81.

Santini, J.-J. (1986). "Les denationalisations au Royaume-Uni," in J.-J. Santini (ed.), *Les privatisations à l'étranger: Royaume-Uni, RFA, Italie, Espagne, Japon*. Paris: La Documentation Française.

Uhel, P. (1986). "La privatisation des entreprises publiques en RFA," in J.-J. Santini (ed.), *Les Privatisations à l'étranger: Royaume-Uni, RFA, Italie, Espagne, Japon*. Paris: La Documentation Française.

United Kingdom National Economic Development Office (1976). *A Study of UK Nationalised Industries*. London:

Vickers, J., and G. Yarrow (1986). "Telecommunications: Liberalisation and the Privatisation of British Telecom," in J. Kay, C. Mayer, and D. Thompson, *Privatisation and Regulation. The UK Experience*. Oxford: Clarendon Press.

Index

About the Contributors

GEORGE L. ATKINS is Vice President, Humana, Inc., Louisville, Kentucky.

BETSY CONRAD is City Clerk, Florence, Kentucky.

ED DOHERTY is Commissioner of Environmental Services, Rochester, New York.

LAWRENCE K. FINLEY, Ph.D., is Associate Professor of Management, Western Kentucky University, Bowling Green, Kentucky.

MARK H. FLENER, J.D., is Assistant Professor, Western Kentucky University, Bowling Green, Kentucky.

PHILIP D. GIANTRIS is President and General Manager, Bird Environmental Systems and Services, Inc., Walpole, Massachusetts.

C. WAYNE HIGGINS, Ph.D., is Professor of Health Care, Western Kentucky University, Bowling Green, Kentucky.

BRUCE JANKEN is City Coordinator, Florence, Kentucky.

LYDIA MANCHESTER is with the International City Managers Association, Washington, D.C.

ROGER F. TEAL, Ph.D., is Professor of Civil Engineering, University of California at Irvine.

JOHN A. TURNER is former Vice President of Rural/Metro Corporation, Scottsdale, Arizona.

JAN PIETER VAN OUDENHOVEN is Professor of Social and Organization Psychology, University of Groningen, The Netherlands.